Cambridge Elements ≡

Elements in Earth System Governance
edited by
Frank Biermann
Utrecht University
Aarti Gupta
Wageningen University
Michael Mason
London School of Economics and Political Science (LSE)

THE NORMATIVE FOUNDATIONS OF INTERNATIONAL CLIMATE ADAPTATION FINANCE

Romain Weikmans
*Finnish Institute of International Affairs
and Université Libre de Bruxelles*

CAMBRIDGE
UNIVERSITY PRESS

CAMBRIDGE
UNIVERSITY PRESS

Shaftesbury Road, Cambridge CB2 8EA, United Kingdom

One Liberty Plaza, 20th Floor, New York, NY 10006, USA

477 Williamstown Road, Port Melbourne, VIC 3207, Australia

314–321, 3rd Floor, Plot 3, Splendor Forum, Jasola District Centre,
New Delhi – 110025, India

103 Penang Road, #05–06/07, Visioncrest Commercial, Singapore 238467

Cambridge University Press is part of Cambridge University Press & Assessment,
a department of the University of Cambridge.

We share the University's mission to contribute to society through the pursuit of
education, learning and research at the highest international levels of excellence.

www.cambridge.org
Information on this title: www.cambridge.org/9781108932073

DOI: 10.1017/9781108943208

First published 2023

A catalogue record for this publication is available from the British Library.

ISBN 978-1-108-93207-3 Paperback
ISSN 2631-7818 (online)
ISSN 2631-780X (print)

The Normative Foundations of International Climate Adaptation Finance

Elements in Earth System Governance

DOI: 10.1017/9781108943208
First published online: February 2023

Romain Weikmans
Finnish Institute of International Affairs and Université Libre de Bruxelles

Author for correspondence: Romain Weikmans,
romain.weikmans@fiiafellow.fi

Abstract: Billions of dollars are annually transferred to poor nations to help them adapt to the effects of climate change. This Element examines how the discourses on adaptation finance of many developing country negotiators, environmental groups, development charities, academics, and international bureaucrats have renewed a specific vision of aid intended to respond to international injustices and to fuel a regular transfer of resources between rich and poor countries. By reviewing manifestations of this normative vision of aid in key contemporary debates on adaptation finance, the author shows how these discourses have contributed to the significant financial mobilization of developed countries towards adaptation in the Global South. But there remains a stark contrast between the many expectations associated with these discourses and today's adaptation finance landscape.

Keywords: adaptation finance, foreign aid, global climate governance, UNFCCC, Paris Agreement

ISBNs: 9781108932073 (PB), 9781108943208 (OC)
ISSNs: 2631-7818 (online), 2631-780X (print)

Contents

1 Introduction

Copenhagen, December 2009. The long-awaited fifteenth Conference of the Parties (COP) to the United Nations Framework Convention on Climate Change (UNFCCC) that was expected to lead to a post-Kyoto global climate agreement ended in a resounding failure of the multilateral climate process. Yet it resulted in the largest financial commitment made to date by developed countries to support developing countries mitigate their greenhouse gas emissions and adapt to the effects of climate change.

Hillary Clinton, then United States' Secretary of State, announced in the ultimate hours of the conference that her country would join other developed countries' proposal to raise US$100 billion annually by 2020 to assist poor countries in addressing climate change (Friedman & Samuelsohn, 2009). Deep disagreements between Parties meant that this announcement was not enough to reach a unanimously agreed decision text. But the Copenhagen financial commitments announced then (UNFCCC, 2009, para. 8) were included in the Cancun Agreements agreed by all Parties one year later (UNFCCC, 2010, paras. 95–99).

The collective commitment by developed countries was 'to provide new and additional resources (. . .) approaching US$30 billion for the period 2010–2012, with a balanced allocation between mitigation and adaptation (. . .)' (UNFCCC, 2010, para. 95). Developed countries also '(. . .) commit[ed], in the context of meaningful mitigation actions and transparency on implementation, to a goal of mobilizing jointly US$100 billion per year by 2020 to address the needs of developing countries' (UNFCCC, 2010, para. 98).

Even if developing country negotiators had asked for four times more than US$100 billion a year (Vidal, 2009), the size of these financial pledges was praised by many academic observers (e.g., Keohane & Victor, 2011; Pickering et al., 2015). The US$100 billion goal appeared rather ambitious when compared to total annual official development assistance (ODA) flows from developed countries, which in 2009 amounted to approximately US$121 billion. This often-made comparison should, however, be qualified as the US$100 billion goal formulated by developed countries aims at mobilizing funding from public and private sources without any specification regarding the respective part of each, while ODA only comprises public financial flows (Weikmans & Roberts, 2019). And such optimism was not shared by everybody. Various civil society organizations considered that 'this amount falls astonishingly short of all reasonable estimates of adaptation and mitigation costs in developing countries' (Fair and Effective Climate Finance, 2010, p. 2).

These financial promises nonetheless remain notable, especially in support of adaptation. Indeed, in international climate negotiations, adaptation had long been considered in an extremely negative light, perceived as a defeatist option, or even seen as competing or distracting from the more important challenges posed by the mitigation of greenhouse gas emissions (Schipper, 2006; Ciplet et al., 2013; Orlove, 2022). High expectations were consequentially associated with these new financial promises towards adaptation, including by academic observers. For some researchers, nothing less than the 'global (re)distribution of wealth' is at play in international efforts to fund adaptation in developing countries (Carmin et al., 2015, p. 169). For others, this issue 'has the potential to transform traditional aid modalities' (Tanner & Allouche, 2011, p. 3). While the success of the adaptation agenda in terms of financial mobilization – or of promises in this regard – is striking, I will show throughout this Element that these different expectations have only materialized to a very limited extent.

According to the Organization for Economic Co-operation and Development (OECD), adaptation finance from developed to developing countries was multiplied tenfold over the last decade, from less than US\$2 billion in 2010 to slightly above US\$20 billion in 2019[1] (OECD, 2021a). Figures compiled by the OECD (2022) suggest that adaptation finance reached an all-time high of US\$29 billion in 2020, despite the COVID-19 pandemic.[2] Yet, in the absence of common accounting rules established under the UNFCCC, these figures – put forward by developed countries – are hotly contested and must be considered with extreme caution (see Weikmans & Roberts, 2019; Roberts et al., 2021). Developing country negotiators have long lamented developed countries' 'inflated' numbers (e.g., Indian Ministry of Finance, 2015). Civil society organizations argue that the 'true' figures represent approximately a third of what the OECD publicizes as adaptation finance (Oxfam, 2020). In any case, developed and developing countries all recognize that the current provision of adaptation finance remains insufficient (see e.g., UNFCCC, 2021, para. 10). Cynical – or realist – observers may, however, point out that COP decisions have over the years regularly 'recognized' this insufficiency of adaptation funding, without offering much prospect for addressing it.

---

[1] These figures do not take into account 'cross-cutting' funding to projects with both mitigation and adaptation benefits, or to climate projects for which the mitigation and/or adaptation benefits were not yet determined at the time of reporting (see OECD, 2021a, p. 7).

[2] Time lags in reporting by developed countries to the UNFCCC Secretariat mean that official climate finance figures for 2020 will not be available before 2023. However, in November 2021, Parties formally recognized and 'note[ed] with deep regret' that the US\$100 billion goal by 2020 had not been met (UNFCCC, 2021, para. 26). In July 2022, the OECD announced that climate finance reached US\$83.3 billion in 2020, falling short by US\$16.7 billion of the intended US\$100 billion target (OECD, 2022).

The debates on adaptation finance do not only address the scale of funds promised and transferred to the Global South. Other contested areas notably concern the sources, distribution, and use of adaptation finance. More broadly, the nature of adaptation finance and its relationship with development aid have also been the source of tensions that remain particularly prominent in international climate negotiations. My primary aim in this Element is to examine the nuances and normative foundations of these longstanding debates.

Such an examination is timely as the landmark Paris Climate Conference of December 2015 saw developed countries signal their intention to maintain the existing US$100 billion mobilization goal through 2025 (UNFCCC, 2015, para. 53). In addition, a higher collective quantified goal from a floor of US$100 billion per year is due to be set before 2025, 'taking into account the needs and priorities of developing countries' (UNFCCC, 2015, para. 53). Unlike the US$100 billion, the post-2025 goal is being negotiated as part of the UNFCCC process. That was a strong demand of developing country negotiators who hope that the new goal will be based on some sort of analysis of needs,[3] rather than being presented as a last-minute political bargaining chip by rich countries. It remains to be seen whether this hope will materialize. In any case, formal negotiations on this post-2025 goal has gotten off to a whirlwind start at COP26 in November 2021 when the Like-Minded Developing Countries – including, among others, China, India, Indonesia, Pakistan, and Saudi Arabia – and the African Group – made up of 54 countries from the African continent – put forward a joint proposal that would require developed countries to mobilize 'at least' US$1,300 billion per year by 2030 to fund mitigation and adaptation activities in developing countries, with a 50–50% balance between both types of activities (LMDCs & African Group, 2021, p. 2). There is therefore little doubt that climate finance will remain one of the crucial issues of multilateral climate negotiations for years to come.

As some readers may not be familiar with the topic, I will first briefly highlight the main contrasting positions generally expressed on the nature and governance of adaptation finance in international negotiations under the UNFCCC (Section 1.1). I will also describe the current landscape of international adaptation finance (Section 1.2) so that every reader is fully equipped

---

[3] In 2018, the COP tasked the Standing Committee on Finance with determining every four years the needs of developing countries in implementing the Convention and the Paris Agreement (UNFCCC, 2018a, para. 13). Its first report on this issue (UNFCCC SCF, 2021b) shows that costed needs for adaptation activities put forward by developing countries in their Nationally Determined Contributions and in their National Communications amount respectively to US$835 billion and US$3,882 billion (over various time scales and using multiple costing methods, often with limited transparency).

to start exploring these controversies in depth. In Section 1.3, I will detail the aims, structure and scope of this Element.

1.1 Contestations on Adaptation Finance: A Primer

Developed and developing countries do not form two perfectly united blocks in international climate negotiations – quite the contrary. On various issues, strong divisions persist within these two groups (see e.g., Vihma et al., 2011; Ciplet et al., 2015; Klöck et al., 2021). Yet, a number of positions are also shared by each of these two groups of countries on climate (adaptation) finance. Let us highlight some of the most prominent ones.

Delegates from most developing countries – supported by many global development charities and environmental non-governmental organizations (NGOs) – generally argue that international climate finance should be treated differently from development aid (Pickering et al., 2015). For many of them, climate finance is owed to developing countries as a form of compensation for the disproportionate responsibility of developed countries for climate change (Roberts & Parks, 2006; Khan et al., 2020). For these actors, the different nature of climate finance – as opposed to development aid – has a number of implications. The most obvious one is that the financial transfers for climate action should be additional to existing development aid commitments – including the long-standing target of devoting 0.7% of donors' national income to ODA (Stadelmann et al., 2011). For this additionality to be truly assessed, developing country negotiators often argue that climate finance should flow through distinct channels – rather than through the ones used for development aid (see e.g., Indian Ministry of Finance, 2015). Developing countries' preferred channels are the funds established under the Convention that give them greater representation in decision-making, for example, through boards with an equal number of representatives from developed and developing countries (Ciplet et al., 2015).

Developing country negotiators have generally insisted that international climate finance should be delivered in a way that reflects their 'right' to receive this funding (Pickering et al., 2015). According to them, this means that climate finance should be delivered as directly as possible to developing countries, without going through international development aid intermediaries such as the World Bank. Such financing should be provided with the fewest conditionalities attached. Moreover, these actors generally push for climate finance to take the form of grants rather than loans, and to equally target adaptation (perceived as providing mainly local benefits) and mitigation (presented as providing primarily global benefits) (see e.g., G77 & China, 2015).

By contrast, developed country negotiators often highlight the complementarities between combating climate change and promoting socio-economic development (Pickering et al., 2015). Many of them see traditional development aid as the vehicle to fulfil climate finance promises. They usually justify the existence of international climate finance by the 'trade-off' that it would be provided in exchange for mitigation action from developing countries. They also frequently insist that the funds transferred should be transparently and efficiently used. Developed country representatives often stress the fact that public climate finance should have a catalytic role in unleashing greater amounts of private finance as the investments needed to shift to a low greenhouse gas emissions and climate-resilient development pathway are in the order of trillions of US dollars, rather than billions (Pauw, 2017; Bodle & Noens, 2018). Another recurring demand expressed by developed countries concerns the broadening of the base of countries contributing to international climate finance efforts (see e.g., Council of the European Union, 2020, para. 6).

It is significant to highlight that many of these positions appear in various unanimous decisions adopted by the COP. For example, developed countries' commitment to mobilize jointly US$100 billion by 2020 is presented 'in the context of meaningful mitigation actions [to be undertaken by developing countries] and transparency on implementation' (UNFCCC, 2010, para. 98). Another example is that climate finance is supposed to be distributed in a 'balanced' manner between adaptation and mitigation (UNFCCC, 2010, para. 95).

However, these points of agreement between developed and developing countries should not obscure the deep divisions that persist regarding their practical implementation. Indeed, most of the features of these pledges have been expressed in very vague terms (Roberts et al., 2021). There is, for example, no agreement on what 'balanced' means in the phrase 'with balanced allocation between mitigation and adaptation'. Does it mean that 50% of climate finance should go to adaptation? Does it mean that more resources could go to mitigation in the short term if more resources are invested in adaptation in the longer term? The same applies to the principle that a 'significant share' of 'new multilateral funding for adaptation' should be channelled through the Green Climate Fund (UNFCCC, 2010, para. 100). Or to the provision that adaptation funding 'will be prioritized for the most vulnerable developing countries, such as the Least Developed Countries, Small Island Developing States and Africa' (UNFCCC, 2010, para. 95). Indeed, how should funding be allocated between countries in these three categories? Beyond these three categories of countries, what are the other 'most vulnerable developing countries'? Should countries whose economies are highly dependent on hydrocarbon exploitation also be considered 'particularly vulnerable' and receive funding for their adaptation to a low-carbon world? There is a lack of agreement on these issues, both between and within developed and developing countries.

Similarly, there is no agreement on what the terms 'new and additional' mean, including among European Union member states and among OECD Development Assistance Committee (DAC) countries. The sources of international climate finance are equally unclear: It is supposed to come from 'a variety of sources, public and private, bilateral and multilateral, including other sources of funding' (UNFCCC, 2010, para. 99). Other examples of what negotiators often call 'constructive ambiguities' (i.e., vague terminologies that lead to consensus between Parties) include words such as 'scaled-up, adequate and predictable funding' (UNFCCC, 2010, para. 97).

In practice, decisions adopted under the UNFCCC leave extreme discretion to developed countries on how to meet their financial commitments (Roberts et al., 2021). The current approach to the governance of climate funding does not much differ from the one that dominates today at the international level for the mitigation of greenhouse gas emissions (Weikmans, 2017). In both cases, the efforts made by the planet's countries are determined by the willingness of each state to act, rather than by its responsibility for climate change or by its financial, institutional and technological capabilities. In the case of mitigation as for international climate finance, a series of global objectives have been decided under the aegis of the UNFCCC (such as the 1.5- or 2-degree limit on global warming and the US$100 billion annual mobilization goal). In both cases, there is no formal sharing of the burden of efforts to be carried out in order to reach these goals.

Just as each country determines the scope and form of its emission reduction policies, so too does each country has full discretion over the financial resources that it gives to support mitigation and adaptation in developing countries. It is up to each developed country to decide why the climate finance it provides can be considered 'new and additional'. Each developed country also defines the sources (public and private) and channels (bilateral and multilateral) of its climate funding, as well as the financial conditions (grants, concessional or non-concessional loans) it offers to beneficiary countries. As I will show below, the international climate (adaptation) finance landscape is therefore profoundly shaped by the decisions made by each developed country.

1.2 The Landscape of International Climate Adaptation Finance

Describing the current climate finance landscape is particularly challenging as there is no agreement under the UNFCCC over what counts as climate finance

(Weikmans et al., 2020b). Developed countries have always resisted calls from developing country negotiators and civil society observers for a multilaterally agreed definition of climate finance. Despite years of discussion towards more standardization – both under the UNFCCC and in other fora such as the OECD DAC – developed countries still use a wide variety of accounting and reporting approaches (Weikmans & Roberts, 2019; see also UNFCCC SCF, 2021a). In addition, many data gaps persist as some countries do not entirely follow the climate finance reporting guidelines agreed under the UNFCCC (Ciplet et al., 2018; Weikmans & Gupta, 2021). Any comparison or aggregation of the data reported by developed countries to the UNFCCC Secretariat – or to other institutions such as the OECD or the European Commission – should therefore be considered with the utmost circumspection.

The governance of climate finance – including on issues related to burden-sharing and allocation between different countries – remains weakly coordinated (Lundsgaarde et al., 2021). This is despite the creation in 2010 of the UNFCCC Standing Committee on Finance which was tasked with advising the COP on how to improve the coherence and coordination of climate finance (Pickering et al., 2017). Developed countries' approaches to delivering climate finance are extremely diverse. Let us illustrate this by considering 2018 climate finance flows as reported to the UNFCCC by developed countries through their Fourth Biennial Reports.[4]

While most international climate finance came from public (91%) rather than private (9%) sources in 2018, some countries heavily relied on the private sector to fulfil their climate finance commitments. A significant portion of climate finance reported by the Netherlands (39%), Denmark (35%) and the United Kingdom (27%) came from private sources in 2018. A huge diversity of approaches can also be observed with regards to public climate finance. While some countries, like the Netherlands or Australia, provided their public climate funding exclusively in the form of grants, other countries mainly provided theirs in the form of loans, guarantees, or export credits. Japan and France, for example, only provided respectively 3% and 9% of their climate finance in the form of grants in 2018. Some donor countries disbursed most of their funding through multilateral organizations (such as Belgium, which channelled 66% of its climate funding via multilateral institutions in 2018). Other countries predominantly rely on bilateral channels (Japan, for example, supplied over 98% of its climate funding through these channels in 2018). Donor countries generally preferred to allocate their funding to mitigation rather than

---

[4] More recent official data on climate finance flows will not be available before 2023 as developed countries are only required to report on 2019 and 2020 flows through their Fifth Biennial Reports to be submitted to the UNFCCC Secretariat by the end of 2022.

adaptation (on average: 70% versus 30% in 2018). This is very clearly the case for Norway (87% for mitigation in 2018) and Japan (84%). In contrast, some developed countries directed most of their support towards adaptation. This is particularly the case for Belgium (75% for adaptation in 2018). The allocation of funding to various sectors and geographical areas also significantly differs between provider countries. While Australia, for example, focused strongly on the island states of the Pacific, Japan provided most of its funding to South-East Asian countries.

Let us now specifically examine the adaptation finance landscape that emerges from the aggregation of each developed country's climate finance approach. What is commonly referred to by developed countries as adaptation finance mainly comes from public sources. According to the OECD (2022), private adaptation finance mobilized by developed countries' interventions accounted for less than 4% of overall adaptation finance in 2016–2020. However, it is important to mention that the tracking of private adaptation finance is still in its infancy (OECD, 2022); several developed countries have never reported to the UNFCCC Secretariat any private adaptation finance mobilized in developing countries (UNFCCC Secretariat, 2020, para. 55).

Most public adaptation finance is directly sourced from developed countries' national treasuries. There is only one exception to this: a 2% share of proceeds of certified emission reductions issued under the Kyoto Protocol's Clean Development Mechanism[5] that is channelled to the Adaptation Fund – one of the four dedicated funds established under the UNFCCC.[6] By June 2022, this represented a somehow modest cumulative total of US$212 million (approximately 17% of the resources available to the Adaptation Fund since its creation, the rest being voluntary contributions) (World Bank, 2022). Despite endless discussions and repeated announcements on these matters, no 'innovative' global public source of climate finance – such as a tax on international financial

---

[5] The Clean Development Mechanism was a flexibility mechanism established by the Kyoto Protocol that allowed developed countries to fund projects that reduced or avoided greenhouse gas emissions in developing countries in order to obtain 'certified emission reductions' that could be used to meet their own national emission reduction targets.

[6] Similarly, a share of proceeds will be levied on the carbon market mechanism established by Article 6.4 of the Paris Agreement in order '(. . .) to assist developing countries that are particularly vulnerable to the adverse effects of climate change to meet the costs of adaptation' (UNFCCC, 2015, art. 6.4). After years of negotiations, Parties agreed that this share of proceeds will be channelled to the Adaptation Fund (UNFCCC, 2018b, para. 5), and that it will notably comprise a levy of 5% on the emission reductions issued under Article 6.4 (UNFCCC, 2021, para. 67). The money that can be expected to flow to the Adaptation Fund thanks to this levy remains unclear at this stage as it will depend on the success of the yet-to-be fully implemented mechanism established by Article 6.4 of the Paris Agreement.

transactions, on fossil fuel extraction, or on international air or maritime transport (see e.g., Müller, 2015) – has been put in place to date.[7]

Public adaptation finance is mainly provided in the form of loans. According to the OECD (2022), loans accounted for 62% of public adaptation finance in 2016–2020. Most of these loans are provided on concessional terms (i.e., extended on terms more generous than market loans).[8] Public adaptation finance almost always qualifies as ODA – and therefore counts towards the well-known 0.7% target of donors' national income to be devoted to ODA. As most developed countries do not reach this 0.7% target, many developing country negotiators and civil society observers argue that a large proportion of reported climate finance cannot be considered 'new and additional' – an accusation frequently rejected by developed countries who have their own understandings of those terms.

The adaptation finance institutional architecture is highly fragmented, with over 60 funds or initiatives supporting adaptation activities in developing countries (NDC Partnership, 2022). According to developed countries' reporting to the UNFCCC, bilateral actors – consisting mainly of bilateral aid agencies and to a far lesser extent of bilateral climate funds – dominate this landscape as they have channelled 89% of adaptation finance in 2018 (UNFCCC SCF, 2021a). Multilateral institutions – such as the World Bank, specialized United Nations agencies and UNFCCC climate funds – have only channelled around 11% of reported adaptation finance during that same year (UNFCCC SCF, 2021a). Figures compiled by the OECD (2022) paint a more balanced picture between bilateral and multilateral channels. However, by any account, the role played by the UNFCCC funds (i.e., the Least Developed Countries Fund, the Special Climate Change Fund, the Adaptation Fund, and the Green Climate Fund) in the adaptation finance landscape appears rather limited. In 2018, these UNFCCC funds approved US$423 million in funding for adaptation projects (UNFCCC SCF, 2021a, p. 75), which roughly represents between 2 and 5% of overall adaptation finance (UNFCCC SCF, 2021a; OECD, 2022). Despite receiving significant political attention and media coverage

---

[7] Another recently discussed innovative source of climate (adaptation) finance consists in the 're-channelling' of some of the US$650 billion in Special Drawing Rights approved by the International Monetary Fund in the summer 2021 to support the global economy in the wake of the COVID-19 pandemic (see Shalal, 2021; Task Force on Climate, Development and the IMF, 2021). It was suggested that some of these SDRs could be re-channelled to a 'Resilience and Sustainability Trust' that would help developing countries combat climate change and improve their health care systems. Such a Trust was still under discussion at the time of writing this Element.

[8] There is limited transparency on the size and conditions of the non-concessional loans that are provided for adaptation to developing countries (Oxfam, 2020; CARE, 2021a) which is why I do not extensively discuss those here.

during international negotiations – and attracting important academic interest – these UNFCCC funds only have a minor role in terms of disbursements.

1.3 Aims, Structure, and Scope of this Element

Most representatives from developing countries, international development charities and environmental NGOs have long been calling for adaptation finance flows that would exist separately from development aid, and that would be distributed 'automatically' and 'directly' (i.e., without conditions and without intermediaries) to the most vulnerable countries. They have also persistently argued that adaptation finance represents a form of compensation related to the historical responsibility of developed countries for climate change. These various actors have been partially joined on these demands by a number of academics (e.g., Ayers & Huq, 2009; Dellink et al., 2009; Gupta, 2009; Barr et al., 2010; Ciplet et al., 2013; Khan, 2015) and multilateral development institutions (e.g., World Bank, 2006, p. 10; UNDP, 2007, pp. 185–98), especially in the years closely preceding and following the Copenhagen climate summit of 2009. Some researchers suggested, for example, that the provision of adaptation finance should be sourced from precisely defined financial contributions made by developed countries, according to their responsibility for climate change and their wealth (e.g., Dellink et al., 2009), and allocated to developing countries according to precise formulaic criteria based on their climate vulnerability (e.g., Barr et al., 2010). However, as shown above, these different characteristics are not observable in the current reality of international adaptation finance.

How can we understand the disconnection between these prominent discourses and observable practices? The central thesis of this Element is that these discourses are the product of a particular vision of what development aid *should be.* My goal in this Element is to reconstruct this specific vision of aid through a careful assessment of four sets of normative questions:[9]

– *Who should be held responsible for the climate-related impacts happening in developing countries?*

> Poverty, lack of infrastructure, climate change, corrupted governments, concentration of people and economic activities in disaster-prone areas: High levels of climate risk in the Global South have many causes. Are developed countries responsible for all these factors? Which of these causes are highlighted by dominant discourses on adaptation finance?

---

[9] These questions are adapted from an analytical framework developed by Jean-David Naudet and his colleagues to analyse the normative dimensions of development aid (see Naudet, 2000, 2006; Jacquet & Naudet, 2006; Naudet et al., 2007).

With what implications for the duty of developed countries to help developing nations? And with what consequences for the nature of their interventions?

– *Why should developed countries provide adaptation finance to the Global South?*

Do dominant discourses stress the existence of a moral duty for developed countries to provide adaptation finance? What are the injustices that adaptation finance should seek to redress? Should adaptation finance only address the effects of climate change? Or should it also tackle other unsatisfying conditions?

– *How should adaptation finance be allocated?*

Should it be prioritized to those who need it the most? Or should it be targeted to those who will make best use of it? Should it be allocated to countries or to individuals? Should recipients be free to use the financial resources provided as they see fit? Or should donors have their say in how their money is spent?

– *How should adaptation finance be evaluated?*

What are the key criteria highlighted by dominant discourses when it comes to judging if adaptation finance plays its role? Is adaptation finance successful only insofar as it effectively reduces the risks posed by climate change? Or is it successful when it transfers large amounts of financial resources from rich to poor countries, no matter how well the money is used? Should adaptation finance rather be assessed based on the extent to which it reaches those countries or individuals that are the most at risk from climate change?

Analysing these four sets of questions will lead to some overlaps; it will also leave some gaps for further examination. But it will allow me to sketch a relatively comprehensive picture of the normative foundations of international adaptation finance, as they can be reconstructed from the analysis of the discourses and practices on this topic.

I will devote a section of this Element to each of the four sets of issues outlined above. For each of them, I will proceed in two steps. I will first present the main normative choices associated with each set of questions. I will then examine how these normative choices are manifest in a series of recurring debates that cut across international adaptation finance. I will conclude in Section 6 by bringing all these normative dimensions together and by briefly outlining a research and policy agenda.

Analysing, as I will do in this Element, the discourses on adaptation finance as manifestations of a specific vision of aid may seem iconoclast or frankly inacceptable to some readers. Many voices from developing country and civil society representatives have repeatedly asserted that *adaptation finance is not aid*. Yet, I will show that the views that these actors hold over *what adaptation finance should be* give a new life to longstanding positions over *what aid should be*. In a way, contrasting the discourses of these actors with the current reality of adaptation finance offers an assessment of their success in terms of pushing for their views and contesting the broader aid realm.

Two important points should be further highlighted before entering the core of this Element. First, the 'discourses' and 'practices' that are the focus of my analyses do not form a clearly definable whole. They vary greatly in scope and nature since I use the term 'discourses' to refer to multilateral development institution's reports, civil society pamphlets, Parties' position papers, academic articles and reports produced by the Intergovernmental Panel on Climate Change (IPCC). I also use the word 'practices' to refer to a diverse set of realities such as the features of multilateral climate funds or to developed countries' adaptation finance accounting methods. Second, my focus in this book is on international adaptation finance. There is, however, no commonly accepted definition of this term, and it means many different things to different people. In this Element, I understand it as the financial flows provided and mobilized by developed countries that derive from their obligations under the UNFCCC to help developing countries adapt to the effects of climate change.

2 Climate Impacts: External or Internal Causes?

Why are developing countries particularly at risk from climate impacts? In the field of development studies, it is common to distinguish between external and internal factors to explain the poverty of nations (e.g., Carr et al., 1998; Naudet, 2000, 2006; Roberts et al., 2014). Here I apply this distinction in an original fashion to the analysis of climate risks faced by developing countries.

Internal causes of climate risks mainly revolve around 'bad' policies or institutions. It could, for example, be argued that the absence or weak enforcement of legislation restricting developments in areas particularly prone to climatic hazards such as floods or cyclones is the main cause of climate risks faced in such areas. When such internal causes are highlighted, the intensity of developed countries' duty to help developing ones is relatively low (see Table 1). Indeed, why should the Global North provide assistance to malfunctioning or even corrupted governments that are responsible for the sufferings of their populations? In addition, if dominant assessments establish that a given country can pull itself out of a situation of high climate risk, it may

Table 1 Normative choices: External or internal causes?

Causes	External causes		Internal causes
	Endogenous to developed countries (e.g., developed countries' disproportionate contribution to climate change, unequal trade rules, legacies of colonization)	**Exogenous to developed countries** (e.g., geographical situations)	(e.g., 'bad' policies or institutions in developing countries)
Developed countries' duty to act	High	Medium	Low

seem necessary to encourage or force it to do so. Developed countries' actions could then be paternalistic or even coercive.

Climate risks faced by developing countries can also be seen as arising from external causes (see Table 1). Geographical situations could be considered as the main causes of climate risks for countries located at low latitudes, where droughts and heat waves are more frequent and pronounced, even without climate change. The feeling of injustice towards such situations is relatively high given that developing countries' exposure to climate impacts is largely out of their responsibility.

Analysts also frequently identify external causes that find their origins in developed countries' actions or inactions. When analysts highlight climate change as the main driver of the high level of developing countries' climate risk, they assign an important duty to act to developed countries – given their disproportionate historical responsibility for climate change. Analysts may also stress a range of non-climatic factors as conditioning the climate risks faced by developing countries. Examples include developed countries' migration policies, international trade rules or legacies of colonization. Analysts that stress these non-climatic factors as primary drivers of developing countries' climate risk similarly assign a large duty to act on developed countries.

Policy responses to these various causes can also be external or internal to developing countries. Analysts could advocate for external responses such as the provision of more adaptation finance from rich countries to help poor countries face the climate shock that is not of their doing. But other actions could also be promoted such as the mitigation of developed countries' greenhouse gas emissions with the prospect of a long-term reduction in the exposure of developing countries to intense levels of climatic stress. Reforms of developed countries' agricultural policies – that could reduce the vulnerability of some countries in the Global South – are yet another example of external responses to the high level of climate risks faced by developing countries.

Mixed diagnoses are also possible: The identification of external causes could lead to the formulation of internal responses. For example, high levels of climate risks could be considered to be mainly due to climate change, but the recommended response could be a reform of the water management policies in a given country.

In the rest of this section, I start by examining the extent to which each of the two ideal-typical assessments presented in Table 1 have dominated international academic and policy discourses on climate change (Section 2.1). I then discuss how these assessments shape developed countries' 'duty' to help poor countries reduce climate risks and how they influence the forms of their actions (Section 2.2).

2.1 Dominant Assessments of Climate Risk

Situations of high climate risk in developing countries often have multiple causes. Stressing one type of causes over others is far from trivial as it inevitably influences developed countries' duty to help developing nations and the forms of their actions. My goal in this subsection is to examine whether one of the two ideal-typical assessments that I have described above dominates over the other in global scientific and policy debates. To achieve this goal, a little detour via the concept of vulnerability is necessary.

Over the past two decades or so, vulnerability has emerged as a central concept in academic research on climate change; it is also widely used in studies and reports published by international institutions on this topic (Ford et al., 2018). Various authors (e.g., Kelly & Adger, 2000; Füssel, 2007; O'Brien et al., 2007) have long highlighted the existence of two interpretations of the word 'vulnerability' in international academic and policy discussions on climate change, distinguishing between an 'outcome' (or 'end-point' or 'biophysical') vulnerability approach on the one hand and a 'contextual' (or 'starting-point' or 'social') vulnerability approach on the other hand. These two interpretations highlight different causes of vulnerability and advocate for different responses to the problem of climate change. I consider them to be almost perfect manifestations in the 'real world' of the two ideal-typical assessments that I have described above.

2.1.1 Outcome Vulnerability and Contextual Vulnerability: Two Standards Assessments

In an outcome vulnerability approach, levels of vulnerability represent the *residual consequences of climate change*; those that persist after adaptation actions have been taken or after forms of adaptation have spontaneously emerged (O'Brien et al., 2007). Vulnerability is then seen as the result of physical impacts of climate change on a given exposure unit – impacts that are partially offset by adaptive responses. Vulnerability assessment is thus the end point of a sequence of analyses that start with the development of greenhouse gas emission scenarios, followed by climate scenarios, biophysical impact studies and finally by the identification of adaptations that may occur or be implemented. Vulnerability can then be expressed quantitatively, for example, as a monetary cost, a change in harvests, in human mortality or in damage to ecosystems. This approach to vulnerability allows the identification of the 'net impact' of climate change. It is particularly relevant for determining the extent to which different greenhouse gas emission scenarios lead to a 'dangerous anthropogenic interference with the climate system' that international efforts to combat climate change have the 'ultimate objective' of preventing (UNFCCC, 1992, art. 2). In this understanding, vulnerability reduction is then primarily achieved through two strategies: first, the mitigation of greenhouse gas emissions in order to reduce the magnitude of climate change; second, the implementation of adaptation measures targeted at projected physical impacts of climate change.

Contextual vulnerability, on the other hand, is seen as the *current or future inability to cope* with external pressures or changes, such as climate change (O'Brien et al., 2007). Vulnerability is then considered as an internal characteristic of socio-ecological systems generated by multiple factors and processes. It is seen as being influenced both by changes in biophysical conditions and by social, economic, political, institutional and technological structures and processes. From this perspective, reducing vulnerability to climate change involves altering the context in which climate change occurs, so that individuals and social groups can respond more appropriately to changing conditions.

These two interpretations of vulnerability are intended, among other things, to meet different needs for information relevant to decision-makers in responding to climate change. It is, for example, crucial to isolate the incremental impact of anthropogenic climate change – by contrasting it with the impact of natural climate variability – to justify greenhouse gas mitigation efforts (Füssel, 2007). It is indeed necessary to have data on the severity of the expected impacts of climate change to 'dose' the mitigation efforts that need to be made. In addition, to determine the extent of possible financial compensations from 'polluters' to 'victims' of climate change impacts, it would also be necessary to isolate the damage attributable to anthropogenic climate change alone. By contrast, while adaptation may require some information on climate change projections, information on the additional impact of anthropogenic climate change is less relevant (see Füssel, 2007; Dessai et al., 2009).

2.1.2 From a Dominant Assessment to Another?

Does one of the two interpretations of vulnerability dominate global scientific and policy debates? In this section, I argue that the outcome vulnerability approach has long dominated climate change research and policy discourses. The UNFCCC text (UNFCCC, 1992) reflects this framing quite clearly. Gradually, however, the contextual interpretation of vulnerability has emerged in international scientific and policy debates (Ford et al., 2018). I argue that the most significant illustration of this emergence is perhaps the change in 2012 of the definition of vulnerability used by the IPCC, from an outcome to a contextual interpretation of this concept.

The UNFCCC: A Founding Understanding of the Climate Problem

When the UNFCCC was drafted, climate change was seen in the same vein as other global environmental problems such as acid rain or ozone depletion (van Gameren et al., 2014). International cooperation was then seen as necessary to mitigate the causes – rather than the consequences – of the pollution (Schipper & Pelling, 2006). The wording of the Convention leaves little room to adaptation; mitigation is *the* response to anthropogenic climate change. The idea was that the effects of climate change could – if mitigation actions were early and vigorous enough – be absorbed by human societies (Schipper, 2006). These societies, provided that catastrophic events could be avoided, would have deployed more or less adequate responses to climate change, without any particular need to anticipate them, as these same societies had always done (Tubiana et al., 2010). The capacity to adapt was therefore considered to be inherent to ecosystems and societies, and therefore did not require any explicit policy (Adger & Barnett, 2009).

This understanding of the climate problem gradually became untenable. By the time of the IPCC Third Assessment Report (IPCC, 2001), it had become clear that mitigation efforts alone would not prevent severe climate impacts, that these impacts would occur more rapidly than expected, and that they would disproportionately affect developing countries (Ayers & Dodman, 2010). Both the understanding of climate change and its magnitude had largely evolved over the course of a decade. Only the first IPCC Assessment Report (IPCC, 1990) was available when the UNFCCC was adopted almost thirty years ago. Since then, the IPCC has summarized the state of knowledge on the subject in six Assessment Reports and has been able to highlight in increasing detail the current and expected impacts of climate change and with increasing certainty the influence of human activities on the climate system.

The outcome vulnerability framing of the text of the Convention (UNFCCC, 1992) is also manifest in the strict distinction that it makes between anthropogenic climate change and natural climate variability. In the climate Convention, 'climate change' is defined as 'a change of climate which is attributed directly or indirectly to human activity that alters the composition of the global atmosphere and which is in addition to natural climate variability observed over comparable time periods' (UNFCCC, 1992, art. 1.2). This definition contrasts significantly with the definition given by the IPCC in its second and subsequent Assessment Reports.[10] The IPCC now defines 'climate change' as

> a change in the state of the climate that can be identified (...) by changes in the mean and/or the variability of its properties and that persists for an extended period, typically decades or longer. Climate change may be due to natural internal processes or external forcings such as modulations of the solar cycles, volcanic eruptions and persistent anthropogenic changes in the composition of the atmosphere or in land use. (IPCC, 1995, p. 21)

The Adoption of a Contextual Understanding of Vulnerability by the IPCC

It is significant to highlight that the definition of vulnerability used by the IPCC in its most recent reports is based on a contextual understanding of the concept – whereas the definition of vulnerability in its earlier reports was based on an outcome approach (see Füssel, 2007).

The most widely accepted definition of vulnerability in the field of climate change had long been that proposed by the IPCC in its Third and Fourth Assessment Reports (IPCC, 2001, 2007) which defined it as 'the degree to which a system is susceptible to, and unable to cope with, adverse effects of climate change, including climate variability and extremes. Vulnerability is a function of the character, magnitude, and rate of climate change and variation to which a system is exposed, its sensitivity, and its adaptive capacity' (IPCC, 2007, p. 89).

In its Special Report entitled 'Disaster and Extreme Event Risk Management for Climate Change Adaptation', the IPCC proposed a more generic definition of vulnerability, understood as 'the propensity or predisposition to be adversely affected' (IPCC, 2012, p. 4). This definition, derived from disaster risk studies,

---

[10] Note that the first IPCC (1990) Assessment Report adopted a definition of climate change similar to the one given in the UNFCCC (1992).

is also the one used in the IPCC Fifth and Sixth Assessment Reports (IPCC, 2014, 2022). It gives a 'fundamentally social connotation' and a 'predictive value' to vulnerability (IPCC, 2012, p. 33). The definition previously used by the IPCC made 'physical causes and their effects an explicit aspect of vulnerability', while the social context was 'considered in the notions of sensitivity and adaptive capacity' (IPCC, 2012, p. 33). In the definition currently used by the IPCC (2012, p. 33), 'vulnerability is considered to be independent of physical events' (i.e., exposure is not a dimension of vulnerability).

This major change in the definition used by the IPCC has only recently started to attract scholarly attention (see Muccione et al., 2017; Sharma & Ravindranath, 2019; Ishtiaque et al., 2022). This is despite the fact that there are numerous references to this term in the UNFCCC text and in COP decisions (for a review, see Klein, 2009). As I will further explore in Section 4, the concept of vulnerability plays an important role in international negotiations on the distribution of adaptation finance.

Does this change in the definition of vulnerability illustrate the predominance of the contextual vulnerability approach in current international scientific and policy discourses on climate change? Rather than the replacement of one dominant approach by another, it is more likely that overlaps between the two approaches can be observed in discourses and practices (Ford et al., 2018; Ishtiaque et al., 2022). I would argue that a partial explanation for this lies in the fact that the issue of adaptation – and its financing – has largely been constructed around the UNFCCC. The text of the Convention, adopted thirty years ago, created the general framework for negotiations in this area. It is therefore plausible that the understanding of both the climate problem and the main responses to it that are apparent in the Convention has had a lasting influence on the processes established under the UNFCCC.

In any case, the change of definition of vulnerability used by the IPCC illustrates the rise of the human and social sciences in the study of climate change. While early IPCC reports focused primarily on characterizing the biophysical impacts of climate change, more recent reports show a progressively more sophisticated understanding of the economic and social impacts of climate change. The domination of the mitigation/biophysical impact approach (outcome vulnerability) has limited the scope of adaptation policies, which have been interpreted in a mostly narrow manner (Khan & Roberts, 2013). This framing still persists among many researchers and decision makers (see e.g., Ishtiaque et al., 2022).

2.2 Responsibilities and Forms of Action

How do the outcome and contextual interpretations of vulnerability relate to the internal versus external dichotomy presented at the start of Section 2? In an outcome vulnerability framing, it is not really the causes of and responses to situations of high level of climate risk that are apprehended, but the causes of and responses to the sole impacts induced by anthropogenic climate change. The causes highlighted in such a framework are highly external to developing countries and largely endogenous to developed countries, since these causes only relate to climate stresses attributable to anthropogenic climate change. In such a framing, developed countries' responsibility is therefore strongly emphasized but only for the fraction of climate impacts that can be attributed to anthropogenic climate change. The main response is situational: reducing climatic stresses through the mitigation of greenhouse gas emissions by high-emitting countries. Adaptive responses are also highly situational. Indeed, they theoretically focus on the 'additional' climate impacts that can only be attributed to anthropogenic climate change – with all the practical difficulties that such a distinction implies.

A contextual vulnerability framework highlights a much wider range of causes of and responses to situations of high level of climate risk. These causes will be situational but exogenous to the international community if high levels of climate risk are perceived to be the consequence of hostile geographies. They will be situational and endogenous to the international community if the diagnosis establishes, for example, that it is European agricultural subsidies that exacerbate climate change vulnerability factors in some African countries. When such causes are highlighted, developed countries' duty to act is strong – and goes far beyond the problem of anthropogenic climate change. Notably, in a contextual vulnerability framing, high levels of climate risk can also be seen as dispositional – that is, as the 'responsibility' of countries facing high levels of climate risk – when 'inadequate' policies or institutions are seen as generating climate risk. In such cases, developed countries' duty to intervene is greatly diminished and their interventions – if they exist – are likely to be based on forms of coercion aimed at inducing governments to change policies or institutions that are perceived as 'problematic'.

2.2.1 Importance and Scope of Adaptation

It is quite fundamental to highlight the fact that the two interpretations of vulnerability reviewed above place very different emphasis on adaptation in the response to climate change. Moreover, the understanding of adaptation is also fundamentally different between these two interpretations.

In an outcome vulnerability framing, the implementation of adaptation actions is only possible on the basis of detailed knowledge on projected impacts of anthropogenic climate change. Both the importance and the scope of adaptation are therefore reduced in this framing. Indeed, adaptation is then fundamentally constrained by the limited availability of sufficiently detailed projections of the physical impacts of climate change that could justify heavy investments in adaptation actions that would specifically aim at responding to a precisely anticipated impact of climate change. When such projections are available, this framing inevitably leads to adaptation being conceived as technological or sectoral changes (e.g., irrigation projects, development of drought-resistant varieties, construction of seawalls).

In a contextual vulnerability framing, on the other hand, the implementation of adaptation actions is possible today since it does not require precise information on projected climate change impacts. Their implementation is also urgent since climate conditions are already placing what is considered to be an unsustainable burden on human development in many developing countries. Adaptation interventions go far beyond actions specifically targeting identified climate change impacts. The 'entry points' for adaptation interventions are multiplied as vulnerability to climate change is seen as emerging from social, political, economic, technological and institutional structures and processes.

2.2.2 Role of Aid

I would argue that the rise of the contextual vulnerability framing in international scientific and policy debates has given a major role in terms of adaptation to 'traditional' development aid interventions. In an outcome vulnerability approach, adaptation aid interventions are quite easily identifiable since they aim specifically to respond to precisely identified impacts of climate change. In a contextual vulnerability framework, on the other hand, the boundaries between adaptation interventions and those of 'traditional' development aid become blurred. Many of these interventions aim in one way or another to act on social, economic, political and/or institutional structures and processes to reduce poverty which, in a multidimensional sense, is seen by many actors as largely synonymous with vulnerability. For example, the landmark report *Poverty and Climate Change: Reducing the Vulnerability of the Poor through Adaptation* (Sperling, 2003) prepared almost twenty years ago by the OECD and nine bilateral, regional and multilateral donors stressed that pro-poor development is the key to effective adaptation. It indicated that many possible interventions had already been identified and that actions could be taken immediately. The proximity between the activities of adaptation finance and development aid has long been highlighted in the academic literature as well (see e.g., McGray et al., 2007; Ayers & Dodman, 2010; Schipper et al., 2020).

This overlap between the main stated aims of development aid – that is, poverty reduction – and of adaptation finance – that is, climate change vulnerability reduction – is quite remarkable. It is, however, problematic if the long-term issues and, above all, the uncertainty of future climate change are insufficiently integrated by traditional development aid actors in their project and programme design (I will further examine this issue in Section 5.2). In any case, bringing together adaptation and development interventions allows traditional aid institutions to play a leading role in international adaptation finance. This leading role is apparent in the landscape of international adaptation finance which as shown in Section 1.2 is largely dominated by bilateral and multilateral development cooperation actors. However, this overlap is the basis for many difficulties in monitoring financial transfers in support of adaptation in developing countries since it is almost impossible to differentiate between adaptation finance and development aid under a contextual vulnerability approach (I will come back to these challenges in Section 5.3). Moreover, this overlap deprives international adaptation finance of its original specificity: financing activities that make it possible to limit the negative effects on human societies and ecosystems of the strictly identified impacts of anthropogenic climate change for which the responsibility and duty to act of developed countries are very strong.

2.3 Conclusion

In this section, I have examined how assessments of the causes of situations of high levels of climate risk inform developed countries' duty to finance adaptation in developing countries. Assessments that highlight external causes that are endogenous to developed countries reveal a maximum duty to act from their part since the recommended responses to such situations are not directly accessible to developing nations. The assessments not only determine the intensity of the duty to act but also influence the nature of the developed countries' interventions.

Assessments that highlight external causes limited to the problem of climate change have long dominated international academic and policy debates. The international climate regime was originally developed to address the challenge of mitigating greenhouse gas emissions. In this context, the concept of adaptation had a very different meaning than the one it currently has. While the bias against adaptation has been largely lifted, this initial conceptualization has had profound impacts on the understanding and treatment of the issue of adaptation at the international level. Assessments of climate risk have gradually highlighted a larger variety of causes. But many assessments still give a fairly central importance to climate-related physical stresses rather than to underlying vulnerability factors (see also Lahsen & Ribot, 2021).

The refined scientific understanding of the determinants of climate risk was influential in shifting dominant assessments towards highlighting more diverse external (i.e., beyond climate change) and internal causes of climate risk. International political dynamics have also likely played a part in that shift. In view of the slow pace of global mitigation efforts, the issue of adaptation finance has rapidly emerged on the agenda of international climate negotiations (Ciplet et al., 2015; Khan et al., 2020). New alliances in the negotiations under the UNFCCC have also been forged, for example, between the European Union and Small Island Developing States – for whom the issue of adaptation finance is of vital importance (Betzold et al., 2012). The perception of an urgency to act in support of developing countries and the search for new justifications for the activities of traditional development aid actors have probably played in favour of a conceptual alignment between adaptation finance and development aid (Weikmans, 2016b).

3 Moral Duty: Distributive or Corrective Justice?

Why do developed countries provide adaptation finance to developing countries? Donors' motivations are undeniably multiple. This section leaves aside the economic and politico-strategic factors that come to play in this (for a discussion see e.g., Ciplet et al., 2015; Weikmans, 2015). My aim here is to clarify the moral justifications for these financial transfers to happen.

Development scholars commonly distinguish between three types of moral duty associated with the provision of development aid (e.g., Opeskin, 1996; Naudet, 2000, 2006). The first type corresponds to the idea that the world is just as it is, and if aid exists, it is based on a principle of charity (without any moral obligations). The second type is linked to a concern for humanism, associated with the perception of a basic level of resources due to each individual. Aid is then aimed at overcoming a level of deprivation that is considered as unacceptable. The third type of moral duty is associated with concerns of justice, which correspond either to the fair distribution of all resources (distributive justice) or to the rectification of precisely delimited injustices (corrective justice). In this section, it is more specifically through these two conceptions of justice that I will analyse adaptation finance provided (or promised) to developing countries. Discourses calling for a strong financial mobilization to help developing countries adapt to climate change are indeed commonly based on these justice dimensions.

What do these two conceptions of justice entail for aid? When based on a distributive conception of justice, aid is justified by a concern to correct a distribution of resources that is unfair in terms of needs or merits (Jacquet & Naudet, 2006). It leads to continuous transfers of resources between those who have more and those who have less than their 'fair share' (Naudet, 2006). By contrast, when based on a corrective conception of justice, aid aims at redressing injustices – not necessarily caused by the Global North – that are precisely identified and situated in time (Naudet et al., 2007). In such a conception, aid can then either compensate the victims of the injustice or redress the situation of injustice as if it had never happened – in order to restore justice once and for all (Naudet, 2006). As Table 2 illustrates, these two principles of justice have different implications for which countries should provide and receive adaptation finance. In Section 3.1 below, I highlight some of the ways in which these justice dimensions are apparent in the negotiations established under the UNFCCC. I then examine illustrations of these dimensions in the debates on the cost of adaptation for the Global South (Section 3.2).

Throughout this Section 3, I do not explore in much detail the procedural dimension of justice. Issues linked to the fair participation of all countries in the governance of adaptation finance are, however, central in international debates on adaptation finance as I will briefly discuss in Section 4 (for a more comprehensive analysis, see Grasso, 2010; Ciplet et al., 2013).

3.1 Distributive and Corrective Conceptions of Justice under the UNFCCC

For many researchers and civil society activists, it is the 'fundamental injustice of climate change' that makes it legitimate for poor countries to receive adaptation finance from developed countries (see e.g., Ciplet et al., 2015; Khan et al., 2020). The rationale is easy to understand: While having contributed little to climate change, poor countries are and will be more affected than rich countries by its adverse effects (Roberts & Park, 2016). Adaptation finance is then considered as a form of compensation, and is sometimes demanded as such by poor and/or low-emitting countries.

However, the issue of compensation for climate damage has always been the elephant in the room of international climate negotiations. Early demands expressed by some developing country negotiators and civil society activists mainly revolved around the concept of 'climate debt' owed by the Global North to the Global South linked to the disproportionate use of the atmospheric space by rich countries (see Martinez-Alier, 2003; Roberts & Parks, 2006; Pickering & Barry, 2012; Khan et al., 2020). For developed countries' negotiators, the

Table 2 Normative choices: Distributive or corrective justice?

	Distributive justice	Corrective justice
Justification of aid	Responding to an unfair distribution of resources	Repairing injustices that are precisely identified and located in time
Purpose of aid	No fixed purpose: continuous transfers of resources between those who have more and those who have less than their 'fair share'	Restoration of the situation of the subject of the injustice as if it had never happened; may lead to compensation
Function of aid	Redistribution	Reparation
Provision of adaptation finance	By those who have more resources than their 'fair share'	By those who are responsible for climate change
Allocation of adaptation finance	To those who have less resources than their 'fair share'	To the victims of climate change

issue of 'compensation' or 'reparation' has always constituted a red line in UNFCCC negotiations (Vanhala & Hestbaek, 2016; Khan et al., 2020). The hypothetical set up of a compensation mechanism for climate damage would also likely face many practical challenges (see e.g., Hallegatte, 2008; Pickering & Barry, 2012). It would indeed require that the damage linked to climate change be clearly identified – and distinguished from those linked to natural climatic conditions. It would also probably imply the assessment in monetary terms of damage to people or to elements that are not commonly traded in markets. In addition to these challenges, in an interstate perspective, it would be necessary to precisely identify the countries responsible and the countries victim of the damage.[11]

In what can be considered a significant development, the landmark Paris Conference led to the formal exclusion of compensation or liability for 'loss and damage' (see UNFCCC, 2015, para. 51). However, this does not mean that any dimension of corrective justice is absent from the Paris Agreement (UNFCCC, 2015), the Convention (UNFCCC, 1992) and various COP decision texts (see Ciplet & Roberts, 2017). On the contrary, dimensions of corrective justice are evident in the mandate of the Least Developed Countries Fund and the Special Climate Change Fund established under the UNFCCC in 2001 to finance adaptation projects in developing countries as these funds are only to cover the 'incremental costs' of climate change (GEF, 2012). In practice, this mandate gives rise to numerous difficulties and contestations related to the identification of the cost component of a given adaptation project that specifically aims at responding to anthropogenic climate change in relation to a *business-as-usual* scenario (i.e., in the absence of anthropogenic climate change) (for an early account, see Ayers & Huq, 2009). Controversies on differentiating climate adaptation from 'normal development' are still very much alive within several multilateral climate funds, including the Green Climate Fund (see Farand, 2021; Singh & Bose, 2021). More than ten years after its creation, the Green Climate Fund still lacks a clear policy on how to approach adaptation costing (GCF, 2021).

More broadly, one of the most striking features of the ethical underpinnings of international adaptation finance under the UNFCCC is the combination of corrective and distributive conceptions of justice (Weikmans & Zaccai, 2017). This is probably best illustrated by the fundamental principle of 'common but

---

[11] Importantly for our argument, the financial transfers that would be claimed or released through such a compensation mechanism would be aimed at compensating for damage, and therefore not at financing adaptation (see also Hallegatte, 2008). However, it could theoretically be envisaged that polluting countries would compensate the would-be victim countries not for the damage done but for the costs of the adaptation actions needed to avoid the damage – before the damage occurs. Such a scheme would probably add an extra layer of complexity to the challenges already mentioned.

differentiated responsibilities and respective capabilities' contained in the Convention (UNFCCC, 1992) and in the Paris Agreement (UNFCCC, 2015). While the terms 'common but differentiated responsibilities' highlight the disproportional contribution of developed countries to climate change, and can arguably be seen as a diluted expression of corrective justice considerations, the principle of 'respective capabilities' is distributive in nature (Weikmans & Zaccai, 2017). In practice, the strong correlation between, on the one hand, responsibility in the occurrence of climate change and, on the other hand, capacity to respond to it has historically made it possible for adaptation finance flows to materialize (see Baer, 2006).

However, a major challenge has gradually emerged: The geography of both responsibility in the occurrence of climate change and financial capacity to respond to it has profoundly changed since the UNFCCC was signed thirty years ago. The economic catch-up of some countries has been achieved at the cost of high greenhouse gas emissions. More than 35 countries considered as 'developing country Parties' under the UNFCCC had in 2019 a gross domestic product *per capita* higher than Bulgaria (the poorest member state of the European Union) (World Bank Open Data, 2022). China has been the world's largest annual greenhouse gas emitter since 2005 (Climate Watch, 2022). In 2018, its emissions were roughly twice those of the United States and accounted for approximately a fourth of worldwide greenhouse gas emissions (Climate Watch, 2022). China's cumulative emissions per capita over 1990–2018 are, however, still more than five times lower than those of the United States (Colenbrander et al., 2021). But eighteen 'developing country Parties' have higher cumulative (over the past three decades) emissions per person than do half of Annex II Parties (Colenbrander et al., 2021).

The differentiation of Parties into fixed categories under the UNFCCC (1992) is probably the clearest application of the 'common but differentiated responsibilities and respective capabilities' principle. Under the UNFCCC (1992), developed country Parties are those included in Annex I to the Convention (i.e., Parties that were members of the OECD in 1992 when the Convention was agreed, as well as countries with economies in transition). Developing country Parties are those not listed in Annex I – therefore commonly referred to as non-Annex I Parties. Under the UNFCCC, only Annex II Parties (a subset of Annex I Parties excluding countries with economies in transition) are formally obliged to provide support to developing country Parties.

While emerging economies such as China and India highlight the differences that persist with developed countries both in terms of responsibilities and capabilities, the latter have long been calling for a broadening of the base of countries that contribute to international climate finance efforts. The Paris

Agreement recognizes this demand and calls on 'other Parties' – beyond Annex II Parties – to provide (or continue to provide[12]) international climate finance on a voluntary basis (UNFCCC, 2015, art. 9.2). While the categorizations established under the UNFCCC (1992) remain unchanged so far, the obligations or expectations associated with various categories of Parties are progressively changing (see also Pauw et al., 2019).

Let us now examine how corrective and distributive conceptions of justice play out in the estimates of adaptation costs for developing countries.

3.2 Distributive and Corrective Conceptions of Justice in the Estimates of Adaptation Costs for Developing Countries

The years immediately preceding the 2009 Copenhagen climate summit saw a sudden proliferation of high-profile studies trying to estimate the cost of adaptation for developing countries. The first of these estimates was published by the World Bank in 2006 (World Bank, 2006). Four other studies then explicitly addressed the same issue in 2007 (i.e., Oxfam, 2007; Stern, 2007; UNDP, 2007; UNFCCC Secretariat, 2007), followed by two others in 2009 (i.e., Project Catalyst, 2009; World Bank, 2009). These studies provided a wide range of estimates, from US$4 billion to US$100 billion per year (over various time scales). While these estimates suffer from significant methodological limitations (see Parry et al., 2009; Fankhauser, 2010; Weikmans, 2012; IPCC, 2014), they were highly cited in the media and certainly played a 'yardstick' role in general expectations around the scale of international financial transfers necessary to cover developing countries' adaptation needs.

The connection is indeed systematically made in these studies between the price tag that they estimate and the amounts expected in terms of international transfers for adaptation.[13] Such a connection is also evident in the Fifth Assessment Report of the IPCC (2014) which stated that 'there is evidence of under-investment in adaptation (UNDP, 2007), with global estimates of the need for adaptation funds variously estimated in the range of US$70 to US$100 billion annually (World Bank, 2009), but with actual expenditures in

---

[12] As of July 2022, ten non-Annex I Parties have for example already contributed (or pledged to contribute) to the Green Climate Fund. These include South Korea (which hosts the Green Climate Fund's headquarters) and Mexico for a total of pledges respectively amounting to US$300 million and US$10 million (GCF, 2022). Other contributions or pledges made by non-Annex I Parties are smaller and sometimes rather symbolic (e.g., Mongolia's total pledges amount to US$0.1 million).

[13] Note that such a connection tends to obscure the fact that, beyond adaptation finance provided by developed countries, significant investments for adaptation are being made in developing countries by domestic governments, private actors, and other developing countries (see e.g., UNFCCC SCF, 2021a, pp. 68–70).

2011 estimated at US$244 million (Elbehri et al., 2011), and in 2012 estimated at US$395 million (Schalatek et al., 2012)' (IPCC, 2014, p. 960). Similar comparisons are also made in each edition of the Adaptation Gap Report published annually by the United Nations Environment Programme since 2014 (see e.g., UNEP, 2021, p. 36). Based on my analysis of these studies, I want to show how several methodological choices made by the authors of these cost estimates illustrate corrective and distributive conceptions of justice.

The estimates published by the World Bank (2006, 2009) and the UNFCCC Secretariat (2007) seem quite clearly based on a logic of corrective justice. Two elements can be highlighted in support of this. On the one hand, these three studies explicitly aim to identify the *additional* adaptation costs induced by climate change *alone*. The considered costs are therefore understood as being distinct from, and additional to, the costs of any other socio-economic development objective, including adaptation to natural climate variability. Somewhat analogously to what I described above in Section 2.1.3, these studies had to determine a baseline against which to measure the costs of adaptation to climate change alone – and thus to quantify the magnitude of the 'adaptation deficit' of developing countries to current climate conditions.

On the other hand, these same studies implicitly or explicitly consider the costs of adaptation as those necessary to cover the actions needed to maintain in the future the levels of climate risk that would prevail without climate change. This means that adaptation is pushed to the point where there is no residual damage from climate change rather than to the point where the marginal costs of adaptation are equal to the marginal benefits of adaptation. This is particularly in line with a corrective conception of justice since such an approach seeks to cover the entire costs of climate change.

Various authors (see e.g., Parry et al., 2009) have criticized this methodological choice by highlighting the fact that the adaptation deficit to natural climate variability in developing countries should also be considered and addressed. This criticism can be linked to a redistributive conception of adaptation finance, then seen as having to respond to multiple injustices and not only to those injustices strictly identified as being related to climate change. Ribot (2010, p. 50), for example, argues that 'adaptation cannot be limited to treating incremental effects from climate change so as to maintain or bring people back to their pre-change deprived state. (. . .) It is this "normal" state that effective climate action must aim to eradicate'.

This argument is well reflected in the approach adopted by the studies published by the United Nations Development Programme (UNDP, 2007) and Oxfam (2007). These two studies cumulate corrective and redistributive dimensions of justice. Indeed, both studies used the figures of the World Bank (2006) study as the basis for their own estimates but added very strong redistributive dimensions to it.

In its 2007/2008 Human Development Report, UNDP (2007) indicates that '(...) rich countries have a moral obligation to support adaptation in developing countries' (UNDP, 2007, p. 198) and highlights the corrective dimension of international financing for adaptation by insisting on the existence of a 'legal principle of compensation' in this area (UNDP, 2007, p. 14). However, the UNDP (2007) adds, in a clearly redistributive vision, that '(...) inequalities in climate change adaptation cannot be viewed in isolation. They will interact with wider inequalities in income, health, education and basic human security' (UNDP, 2007, p. 185). The authors of the UNDP study did not hesitate to add US$40 billion per year by 2015 to the estimate produced by the World Bank (2006) for 'strengthening social protection programmes and scaling up aid in other key areas (...) in ways that build resilience and reduce vulnerability' (UNDP, 2007, p. 194), as well as the cost of 'increasing climate-related disaster relief by US$2 billion per year in bilateral and multilateral aid by 2015 to avoid diversion of development assistance' (UNDP, 2007, p. 194).

Similarly, for Oxfam (2007, p. 4), 'in line with the "polluter pays" principle, [international adaptation finance] is owed not as aid from rich country to poor country, but as compensatory finance from high emissions countries to those most vulnerable to the impacts'. Oxfam (2007) also added redistributive dimensions to these clearly corrective demands. Indeed, the authors of the Oxfam (2007) study added US$7.5 billion per year to the World Bank (2006) figures in order 'for NGOs to provide community-based support for adaptation' (Oxfam, 2007, p. 20).

The methodologies used by the authors of these estimates illustrate the existence of strong corrective and redistributive concerns in the global debate on international adaptation finance prior to the 2009 Copenhagen climate summit. To the best of my knowledge, the exact impact that these studies have had on countries' positions related to adaptation finance at COP15 and beyond has never been thoroughly investigated. Nevertheless, it is likely that developing country representatives benefited from seeing their financial demands legitimized by the adaptation cost estimates carried out by international reference institutions such as the World Bank, UNDP, and the UNFCCC Secretariat.

A very limited number of adaptation cost estimates for developing countries have emerged since 2010 (Hallegatte et al., 2018; Chapagain et al., 2020). Often-cited figures are those contained in the 2016 UNEP Adaptation Gap Report (UNEP, 2016) that put the costs of adaptation for developing countries at US$140–300 billion per year by 2030, and US$280–500 billion by 2050.

There is, however, limited information available on how these numbers were devised beyond the fact that they were based on the World Bank (2009) study discussed above, and adjusted by a factor 4 to 5, based on 'an in-depth review of national and sector cost estimates' (UNEP, 2014, pp. 25–6, 2016, p. xii). We may, however, expect a renewed interest in estimating the costs of adaptation for developing countries in the next couple of months and years as Parties have agreed to set up a new climate finance goal before 2025, 'taking into account the needs and priorities of developing countries' (UNFCCC, 2015, para. 53).

3.3 Conclusion

This section raised the question of the primary purpose of international climate adaptation finance: Is it to restore the situation of countries that are confronted with the injustice of climate change as if it had never happened? Or is it rather about setting up or reinforcing a system of global wealth redistribution so that countries affected by multiples injustices – including those linked to climate change – can better cope with them?

Corrective and distributive conceptions of justice are present in the text of the Convention (UNFCCC, 1992) and in the Paris Agreement (UNFCCC, 2015). A strictly corrective conception of justice is also apparent in the mandates of the Least Developed Countries Fund and the Special Climate Change Fund established under the UNFCCC to finance climate change adaptation projects in developing countries as these funds are only to cover the 'incremental costs' of climate change.

Corrective and distributive justice concerns have also been strongly expressed in the discourse of many actors, including multilateral institutions. Importantly, UNDP and several global development charities have added strong redistributive demands – which they already convey in their daily work – to corrective justice dimensions. For these actors, international adaptation finance should not aim solely or mainly at responding to a clearly identified injustice – that is, the disproportionate responsibility of developed countries for climate change. In their view, climate change provides additional justifications for increased North-South financial transfers to address a multitude of ever-recurring injustices. They consider that the burden imposed by climate change on some countries is an illustration of the permanence and reconfiguration of these longstanding injustices.

Beyond the rhetoric, it is, however, important to highlight the limited impact of corrective and distributive justice considerations on the concrete implementation of international adaptation finance. As highlighted in Section 1.1, more than the responsibility in the occurrence of climate change (corrective justice) or the financial capacity (distributive justice), it is the willingness of each developed country that has so far served as the basis for sharing the burden of adaptation finance efforts. In this sense, international adaptation finance is in practice more a matter of charity or humanism than of justice (see also Hallegatte, 2008; Füssel et al., 2012).

4 Allocation: Liberal or Perfectionist Perspective?

In this section, I distinguish between a liberal perspective and a perfectionist perspective towards the allocation of aid (see Naudet, 2000, 2006; Jacquet & Naudet, 2006). Through the allocation of their aid, to what extent do donors seek to promote specific preferences or development models? The answer to this question determines whether aid falls under a rather liberal or a rather perfectionist perspective.

Under a liberal perspective, aid is automatically allocated according to the objective measurement of certain parameters of the beneficiaries, most often their needs (Naudet, 2006). Recipients can then use the financial resources provided as they see fit. The financial transfer is considered as a right for beneficiaries who meet given eligibility criteria. It is worth noting that most social assistance programmes in welfare states are based on this logic (Jacquet & Naudet, 2006).

By contrast, from a perfectionist perspective, aid is provided within a contractual framework between a donor and a recipient. The latter agrees to carry out specific actions in exchange for the financial resources provided by the donor (Jacquet & Naudet, 2006; Naudet, 2006). The 'contract' between the donor and the beneficiary may imply that the financial resources can only be devoted to specific uses – for example, to build an irrigation project. This modality is often referred to as targeted aid. Other types of contractual arrange-ments are also possible: The donor may provide resources to the beneficiary under the condition that the latter commits to legal or policy reforms (as in the case of budget supports or structural adjustment programmes). In such cases, recipients can use the financial resources as they wish, but at the same time they must follow the directions set by the donor if they want to (continue to) obtain financial resources. This modality is referred to as conditional aid.

The various dimensions of these liberal and perfectionist perspectives are presented in Table 3. These perspectives represent 'ideal-types': Their charac-teristics are not necessarily perfectly observable in practice. A combination of both perspectives is also possible. In what is called 'selective allocation', for example, a donor selects and supports beneficiaries in the implementation of activities of their own choosing. The process of selecting the beneficiaries who

Table 3 Normative choices: Liberal or perfectionist perspective?

	Liberal perspective	**Perfectionist perspective**
Vision	Aid as a right	Aid as an incentive
Allocation	Automatic, according to the needs of beneficiaries	According to a contract between the donor and the beneficiary
Use of financial resources	Free	Restricted to specific uses (targeted aid)
		Free use but other commitments (conditional aid)

will be helped and of determining the support that they will receive will tilt aid towards a rather liberal or a rather perfectionist perspective (Naudet, 2006).

Two further points should be mentioned before examining manifestations of these liberal and perfectionist perspectives in the discourses and practices on adaptation finance. First, the assessments of the causes of high level of climate risk examined in Section 2 often play a role in the allocation perspective that will be adopted by donor countries. When external causes are highlighted, it is likely that aid will be perceived as a right for developing countries, especially if developed countries are deemed to be responsible for these external causes (Naudet, 2006). By contrast, when climate risk assessments stress internal causes, donors will likely lean towards a perfectionist perspective that considers aid as an incentive for the beneficiaries to address those internal causes that are under their control (Naudet, 2006).

Second, the aid literature makes an important distinction between states and individuals as legitimate beneficiaries of aid (see e.g., Beitz, 2000; Chatterjee, 2004). While this distinction will not be the focus of my analysis in this section, some points can, however, be highlighted. Under the UNFCCC (1992), adaptation finance is only framed as an interstate issue. General considerations related to vulnerable groups, communities and individuals appear in several COP decisions and in the Paris Agreement (UNFCCC, 2015, Preamble) but they are not directly linked to adaptation finance. The distinction between states and individuals as legitimate beneficiaries of adaptation finance is nonetheless discussed in the academic literature, notably through a focus on the importance of supporting community-based adaptation (for a review, see Forsyth, 2013). Various studies (e.g., Barrett, 2013) have also focused on the fairness of sub-national adaptation finance distribution (i.e., the extent to which adaptation finance is allocated to the most vulnerable individuals).

4.1 Liberal Discourses versus Perfectionist Practices

A liberal perspective towards the allocation of adaptation finance is evident in the discourses of many developing country negotiators and civil society representatives. These actors have repeatedly stressed that the transfer of adaptation finance from developed to developing countries is a right for the latter and that these financial resources should be allocated to those developing countries that have the greatest needs in this regard – often referred to as 'particularly' or 'most' vulnerable countries (Ciplet et al., 2013; Pickering et al., 2015; Duus-Otterström, 2016; Khan et al., 2020).

These discourses contrast significantly with the practices of dominant adaptation finance providers. While numerous COP decision texts recognize that 'particularly vulnerable countries' should receive adaptation finance in priority, none of these texts provides an operational definition of the term that would make it possible to rank priority recipients of adaptation finance (see Klein, 2009; Harmeling & Kaloga, 2011; Horstmann, 2011; Klein & Möhner, 2011). The lack of clarity on which countries should be prioritized for adaptation funding reflects a lack of consensus on this issue for more three decades among Parties to the Convention, including among developing countries (for an overview of tensions on this issue within the G77 and China, see Khan, 2014, pp. 63–8).

In the current adaptation finance landscape, each developed country remains sovereign over its allocation decisions (Roberts et al., 2021). In the absence of international consensus on which countries should be prioritized – beyond broad categories such as 'Least Developed Countries, Small Island Developing States and Africa' (e.g., UNFCCC, 2010, para. 95) – each developed country has to make decisions on how it allocates its adaptation finance between more than 150 developing countries. As explained in Section 1.2, practices vary tremendously between developed countries in this regard (see also Betzold & Weiler, 2018). A prolific literature has tried to empirically examine the determinants of adaptation finance allocation, such as recipient needs, recipient merits or donor interests (see e.g., Robinson & Dornan, 2017; Weiler et al., 2018). While some researchers found that donors tend to prioritize the most vulnerable (Betzold & Weiler, 2017; Weiler et al., 2018; Doshi & Garschagen, 2020; Islam, 2022), others did not establish this correlation (Stadelmann et al., 2014; Robertsen et al., 2015; Saunders, 2019; Michaelowa et al., 2020; Garschagen & Doshi, 2022; OECD, 2022). Overall, the empirical literature on this topic remains inconclusive: The various indicators and datasets used by analysts as proxies for adaptation finance flows and levels of vulnerability lead to contrasting results.

As highlighted in Section 1.2, the bulk of adaptation finance is channelled through bilateral development agencies and to a lesser extent via multilateral institutions – mainly multilateral development banks such as the World Bank which remain largely controlled by developed countries. Adaptation finance that goes through these channels are always allocated within a contractual framework between a donor and a recipient, so largely lean towards a perfectionist perspective. This perfectionist dimension is softened when beneficiaries are supported in the implementation of projects and programmes that respond to their own needs and priorities. But what are the needs and priorities of developing countries and who determine them?

Under the UNFCCC, National Adaptation Programmes of Action (NAPA) provided a process through which Least Developed Countries were supposed to identify their 'urgent and immediate adaptation needs' defined as those for which 'further delay could increase vulnerability, or lead to increased costs at a later stage' (UNFCCC, 2001b, Preamble, Annex, para. 1). Submitting a NAPA to the UNFCCC Secretariat was necessary to be able to apply for funding under the Least Developed Countries Fund. A prolific academic literature has highlighted the difficulties and limitations linked to this process (see e.g., Ayers, 2011; Holler et al., 2020). Many researchers stressed the fact that these documents, which were supposed to be 'owned' by beneficiary countries, were sometimes produced through very limited stakeholder consultation processes.[14] More broadly, adaptation project proposals and strategic documents such as National Adaptation Plans – through which countries are supposed to identify their medium- and long-term adaptation needs (see UNFCCC, 2011) – remain very often drafted or heavily influenced by international consultants who master the international rhetoric and the various funding requirements in this area (see e.g., Shankland & Chambote, 2011; Falzon, 2021). These elements further reinforce the perfectionist dimensions towards the allocation of aid highlighted above.

By contrast, the allocation practices of some of the dedicated climate funds established under the UNFCCC tend to reflect a liberal approach towards the allocation of aid. These climate funds only play a minor role in the current adaptation finance landscape but their institutional features are worth examining as they profoundly differ from the ones of the other funding channels.

---

[14] It should also be noted that the legitimacy of the elites of some developing countries to negotiate and implement international adaptation finance's arrangements is regularly questioned (see e.g., Tellam et al., 2018). Lynas (2015) for example suggested that developing countries that 'slip backwards into autocracy and corruption should be excluded from accessing the US$100 billion climate finance promised to developing nations'.

4.2 Multilateral Funds' Distinctive Allocation Approaches

Some observers (e.g., Barr et al., 2010; Feindouno et al., 2020) have long been calling for the implementation of 'objective and empirically measurable benchmarks' to guide a 'transparent, equitable and efficient distribution' of adaptation finance resources (Barr et al., 2010, pp. 843–4). However, the current allocation methods of multilateral adaptation funds are not based on such formulas. This contrasts, for example, with the distribution of mitigation resources by the Global Environment Facility (GEF)[15] which allocates its funding based on the 'System of transparent allocation of resources' (STAR) – a system that determines the amount of money a country is eligible to receive during the period covered by a GEF replenishment[16] (see GEF, 2018).

It is difficult to determine a priori whether the use of an allocation formula to distribute adaptation finance would fall under a liberal or a perfectionist perspective. The dimensions of such a formula could largely prove to be perfectionist if they prioritize countries based on their past or future performance. The International Development Association – the part of the World Bank that helps the world's poorest countries – uses a Resource Allocation Index to determine the allocation of its resources among eligible countries. By using such an index, the World Bank has been criticized for indirectly imposing a single development model to all countries (Kanbur, 2005). This Index is indeed supposed to capture 'each country's performance in implementing policies that promote economic growth and poverty reduction' (IDA, 2022). The 'policies' in question are precisely those recommended by the Bank – which therefore knows the 'right development model' that countries should follow (see Charnoz & Severino, 2015, pp. 109–10). By contrast, a formula with fully transparent needs assessment criteria would be part of a liberal approach to aid allocation.

In practice, the different multilateral adaptation funds have adopted various approaches to the allocation of their resources. Significantly, all multilateral funds – whether established under the Convention or not – have sought to incorporate into their allocation processes the principle of prioritizing the most vulnerable countries. In the rest of this section, I mainly analyse the allocation practices of the Adaptation Fund, which is widely considered in

---

[15] The GEF also supports adaptation activities but exclusively through its Least Developed Countries Fund and its Special Climate Change Fund. The STAR is not used by any of these two funds.

[16] The calculation of this amount involves indices that notably measure a country's potential to contribute to global environmental improvement, the performance of GEF implemented projects, and a country's commitment to put in place environmental policy and institutional reforms (see GEF, 2018).

the academic literature as a 'laboratory' of international adaptation finance efforts (see de Guio & Rencki, 2011).

Since its inception (and as of June 2022), the Adaptation Fund has received contributions amounting to US$1,235 million (World Bank, 2022). This figure includes US$212 million obtained through the 2% levy on the share of proceeds of certified emission reductions issued under the Kyoto Protocol's Clean Development Mechanism, and contributions of US$514 million from Germany (where the Fund has its headquarters). The Fund has approved funding proposals for more than US$1 billion and has disbursed more than US$600 million to 132 projects and programmes in more than 100 countries. The future of the Adaptation Fund appears quite rosy. It raised a record US$365 million in new pledges at COP26 in Glasgow in 2021, including first-time contributions from the United States and Canada (Adaptation Fund, 2021c). As highlighted in Section 1.2, Parties also agreed in Glasgow that a levy of 5% on the emission reductions issued under Article 6.4 of the Paris Agreement will be channelled to the Adaptation Fund (UNFCCC, 2021, para. 67).

But the history of the Adaptation Fund has not been a long, quiet river. Established in 2001 to finance 'concrete adaptation projects and programmes' in developing country Parties to the Kyoto Protocol 'that are particularly vulnerable to the adverse effects of climate change' (UNFCCC, 2001a, para. 1, 2007, para. 1), it only became operational eight years later, in 2009. Following the collapse of the price of certified emission reductions issued under the Clean Development Mechanism – from US$20 in 2008 to less than US$3 in 2012 – the Adaptation Fund saw its funding dropped dramatically (Weikmans, 2015). Some European countries recapitalized the Fund several times over the years. As the Kyoto Protocol's second commitment period was due to end in 2020, intense debates occurred on the future role – if any – that the Adaptation Fund would have under the Paris Agreement (for a detailed account, see McGinn & Isenhour, 2021). COP21 in Paris in 2015 decided that the Fund 'may' serve the Agreement (UNFCCC, 2015, para. 59), but difficult negotiations continued until 2018 when Parties finally agreed that the Adaptation Fund 'shall' serve the Paris Agreement (UNFCCC, 2018b, para. 1). These negotiations were characterized by extremely vocal and almost unanimous support from developing countries for the future of the Adaptation Fund under the Paris Agreement. This support cannot be overstated, developing countries really made it clear that the Adaptation Fund was absolutely crucial for them, and 'crafted a narrative that the future of global climate adaptation rested on the shoulders of a continued Adaptation Fund' (McGinn & Isenhour, 2021, p. 7).

This massive support expressed by developing countries for the Fund can largely be explained by its institutional features – that developing country negotiators wanted to keep at all costs. In the crowded landscape of adaptation finance, the Adaptation Fund differs from other multilateral climate funds in four central aspects (Harmeling & Kaloga, 2011; Weikmans, 2015). First, the Board of the Adaptation Fund is composed of a majority of representatives from developing countries (11 out of 16 seats). Each member of the Board has one vote, with decisions being taken by a two-thirds majority when consensus is not possible. This primacy given to developing countries in the governance of the Adaptation Fund is unique in the international climate finance landscape.

Second, as highlighted in Section 1.2, the financing of the Fund was supposed to rely heavily on an international tax of 2% on the 'carbon credits' issued under the Clean Development Mechanism, in order to avoid making the Fund dependent on voluntary contributions from developed countries. Developing countries arduously fought for a similar mechanism under the Paris Agreement – that is the levy of 5% on the emission reductions issued under Article 6.4 of the Paris Agreement mentioned above.

Third, the Adaptation Fund was the first multilateral climate fund that implemented a 'direct access' modality that allows beneficiary countries to submit their requests for funding to the Adaptation Fund without going through the 'filter' of traditional development institutions such as the World Bank or UNDP. A maximum of 50% of the Fund's resources can be channelled through multilateral implementing agencies – the other 50% must be channelled through national implementing agencies – precisely to encourage this direct access modality.

Fourth, the Adaptation Fund was designed with the mandate to finance the 'full cost' of 'concrete adaptation projects and programmes'[17] – rather than the 'incremental cost' of climate change adaptation that some other multilateral climate funds are to cover. This was a strong demand from developing country representatives who were deeply dissatisfied with the difficulties to get access to the resources of these other funds (Ayers & Huq, 2009; Harmeling & Kaloga, 2011).

These four aspects tend to place the Adaptation Fund in a much more liberal perspective of aid than the other multilateral climate funds. As explained by Harmeling and Kaloga (2011), '(. . .) the key reasons for the developing

---

[17] A 'concrete adaptation project' is defined as 'a set of activities aimed at addressing the adverse impacts of and risks posed by climate change. The activities shall aim at producing visible and tangible results on the ground by reducing vulnerability and increasing the adaptive capacity of human and natural systems to respond to the impacts of climate change, including climate variability' (Adaptation Fund, 2021b, p. 3).

countries to fight for the independent Fund [at the time of its creation] were (. . .) the desire for establishing structures independent of the conventional, donor-driven finance architecture, including based on the argument that adaptation is rather restitution than development aid (. . .)' (p. 25). The uniqueness of the Adaptation Fund can be explained by the fact that the United States could not heavily influence its development as the Fund was created under the Kyoto Protocol that the United States never ratified (Ciplet et al., 2013).

However, in a similar fashion as all the other multilateral climate funds, the Adaptation Fund has an allocation approach based on selectivity: Eligible countries must submit project and programme proposals, which are then assessed by the Fund's Board. Financial resources are therefore not allocated 'automatically' to beneficiary countries according to their needs. Furthermore, beneficiaries can only use the financial resources that they receive to implement strictly defined projects and programmes. As noted above, selectivity lies in an intermediate position between a liberal and a perfectionist perspective towards the allocation of aid. Let us examine whether the Adaptation Fund's approach leans towards one or the other.

How does the Adaptation Fund choose the projects and programmes that it supports? The Fund's resource allocation approach was set by Parties in a decision on its 'Strategic Priorities, Policies and Modalities' (UNFCCC, 2008, Annex IV). Most of these 'Strategic Priorities, Policies and Modalities' are not defined in a directly operationalizable manner (Stadelmann et al., 2014; Persson & Remling, 2014), which has left considerable discretion to the Board on how to implement them. This document, for example, defines eligible countries as 'developing country Parties to the Kyoto Protocol that are particularly vulnerable to the adverse effects of climate change, including low-lying and other small island countries, countries with low-lying coastal areas, arid or semi-arid areas, or areas liable to floods, drought and desertification, as well as developing countries with fragile mountain ecosystems' (UNFCCC, 2008, Annex IV, para. 10). This wording – which is identical to the one contained in the preamble to the Convention (UNFCCC, 1992) – does not make it possible to target priority recipients among developing countries as almost all of them fall under such a broad definition of 'particularly vulnerable' countries (Harmeling & Kaloga, 2011; Horstmann, 2011; Klein & Möhner, 2011).

The Board of the Fund intensively discussed the issue of vulnerability at various meetings and invited a number of academic experts to reflect on this matter (Klein & Möhner, 2011). However, the Board decided that it would not adopt a more operational definition of vulnerability than the one formally given in its 'Strategic Priorities, Policies and Modalities'. Thus, no list of countries that are or are not 'particularly vulnerable' was established. In practice, all the developing country Parties to the Kyoto Protocol were considered eligible – which represents more than 150 countries.

The universal eligibility of countries to apply for funding from the Adaptation Fund is well in line with a liberal perspective towards the allocation of aid. However, crucially for our discussion here, the work of several academics has highlighted the lack of prioritization by the Fund's Board of the project and programme proposals submitted by eligible countries (Stadelmann et al., 2014; Persson & Remling, 2014; Remling & Persson, 2015). Project or programme proposals are not compared with each other. When they do not get approved, they can be resubmitted later. In practice, proposals are thus accepted on a first-come, first-served basis, provided that the amount requested does not exceed a 'country cap' and that the proposal is judged to be of 'sufficient technical quality' by the Fund's Board. Let us examine these two dimensions.

The country cap – set by the Board – is the maximum amount that can be allocated to each country by the Fund. It had long been set at US$10 million but it was raised to US$20 million[18] in April 2021 (Adaptation Fund, 2021a). This egalitarian approach to setting a country cap is largely inequitable since the financial resources provided to beneficiaries are not modulated according to their level of needs. It seems obvious that populous countries such as India or the Democratic Republic of Congo have larger needs than sparsely populated states such as Botswana or Mongolia. In addition, countries that do not have sufficient institutional capacity to apply for funding are simply excluded, even though they are potentially very vulnerable to climate change. Recognizing this second difficulty, the Adaptation Fund has been providing capacity-building support through its 'Readiness Programme for Climate Finance' since 2014. However, various LDCs in Africa and conflict-ridden states have still not received any funding from the Adaptation Fund, probably due to weaknesses in the government institutions of those countries.

The 'technical quality' of proposals submitted to the Adaptation Fund is assessed by the Board in light of the Adaptation Fund's 'Strategic Priorities, Policies and Modalities' mentioned above, as well as other documents – approved by the Board – that operationalize them. For example, the 'Instructions for Preparing a Funding Application' (Adaptation Fund, 2017) state that 'the project/programme activities (...) should be distinguished from a "business-as-usual" development or environmental protection project by clearly demonstrating that the proposed adaptation measures are suited or

---

[18] It is important to note that 'individual country project requests are kept to a maximum of US$10 million each. Countries must also have either spent at least US$8 million or last accessed funding at least four years ago in order to access the increased funding limit of US$20 million' (Adaptation Fund, 2021a).

adequate for the identified climate threats. The project/programme proposal should therefore explain the project rationale in relation to the climate scenario(s) outlined in the background and context section (...)' (Adaptation Fund, 2017, pp. 4–5). This climate-centric approach is problematic for several reasons (see Section 2.2.1; see also e.g., Weikmans, 2013; Ledant, 2016; Singh & Bose, 2021) but for the sake of my argument here, it is important to highlight that beneficiary countries do not have full discretion over the design of the projects and proposals that can be funded. This perfectionist approach is further reinforced by the fact that proposals can be submitted in two phases, with feedback from the Fund Secretariat after the first phase. Proposals submitted using this two-phase approach are more often approved than those submitted directly in full form (Adaptation Fund, 2011).

What can we conclude from this short review? The institutional design and allocation practices of the Adaptation Fund clearly reflect a rather liberal approach towards the allocation of aid. However, four key dimensions take it away from the purest form of liberal approach described at the start of Section 4. First, financial support is not automatically allocated to beneficiaries; countries have to formally submit a project or programme proposal to the Fund. Second, beneficiaries are not free to use the money they receive from the Adaptation Fund as they pleased; financial resources can only be used to implement the agreed project or programme proposal. Third, while the Fund supports beneficiary countries in their own projects and programmes, its application guidelines influence the types of projects and programmes that are submitted. Fourth, the Fund does not modulate the support that it provides according to the needs of beneficiaries. It is, however, important to recall that these various dimensions have been negotiated between developed and developing country representatives, and that developing countries have a majority of seats at the Adaptation Fund's Board, which arguably soften the perfectionist nature of these allocation practices.

4.3 Conclusion

The discourses of many developing country negotiators and civil society representatives clearly convey demands that fall under a liberal perspective towards the allocation of aid. However, a very strong dose of perfectionism permeates the practices of most adaptation finance providers. Financial resources are not 'automatically' allocated to recipient countries according to transparent criteria of need. Recipient countries are generally not free to use these resources beyond the implementation of strictly defined projects and programmes. When they are, they must commit to implementing other actions, such as climate policy changes as in the case of the direct budget supports provided to Vietnam by various donors (see Weikmans, 2015). In addition, there is a significant lack of transparency on how most donors select beneficiaries and determine the intensity of support that is to be provided to them. When dimensions of these processes are made explicit (such as for some multilateral climate funds), they fundamentally influence the formulation of project and programme proposals submitted for funding.

Furthermore, a perfectionist dimension accompanies 'by definition' international adaptation finance flows insofar as they specifically aimed at supporting or encouraging adaptation in developing countries. Two points should be highlighted here. First, this perfectionist dimension will have relatively limited effects under a broad interpretation of adaptation (see Section 2.2.1). Under such a broad interpretation, adaptation interventions go far beyond those that target precisely identified impacts of anthropogenic climate change. This interpretation blurs the distinction between 'adaptation' and 'development' projects (see e.g., McGray et al., 2007; Ayers & Dodman, 2010; Schipper et al., 2020). Second, this perfectionist dimension paradoxically emerges from a recurring demand expressed by developing country representatives in international negotiations: to be able to make a strict distinction between international adaptation finance, on the one hand, and international development finance, on the other hand.

5 Evaluation: Deontological or Consequentialist Attitude?

The question of evaluation – already largely present in the dimensions previously examined – sheds additional light on the foundations of the recurring debates on international adaptation finance. In this section, I distinguish between a deontological and a consequentialist attitude, as conceptualized by several development aid theorists (Opeskin, 1996; Clarke, 1999; Naudet, 2000, 2006).

A deontological attitude leads to the legitimization of aid as a principle, regardless of its consequences. Two evaluation criteria are often associated with such an attitude: first, the financial efforts made by developed countries: the larger the financial transfers, the more aid plays its role, regardless of its ultimate consequences; second, the fairness of resource allocation: Aid must be distributed according to the needs (or merits) of beneficiaries. While the financial transfer is legitimate in itself, it can nevertheless be associated with different objectives such as improving living conditions, or financing investments. However, no direct link is made between the scale of the financial transfer and the achieved results. Under a deontological attitude, it can therefore be justified to fund unprofitable projects. By contrast, a consequentialist attitude leads to the

Table 4 Normative choices: Deontological or consequentialist attitude?

	Deontological attitude	**Consequentialist attitude**
Evaluation criteria	Donor countries' financial effort	Efficiency in producing results
	Fairness of resource allocation	Sustainable, persistent impact
Underlying logic	Aid as a financial transfer	Aid as an investment

evaluation of aid with regards to the objectives that are set for it. Aid can then only be justified by the achievement of its results and their sustainability (i.e., their persistence). The main dimensions of these two attitudes are summarized in Table 4.

Global discourses on development aid are profoundly enshrined in a consequentialist attitude (Naudet et al., 2007), as evidenced by the importance given to the issue of aid effectiveness (OECD & UNDP, 2019; Brown, 2020). Most discourses on international adaptation finance contrast significantly with such an attitude as they tend to focus on the scale of financial resources (to be) made available to developing countries and on the importance of their allocation to those most in need. UNDP's *Human Development Report* entitled 'Fighting climate change: Human solidarity in a divided world' (UNDP, 2007) offers a vivid illustration of such a deontological attitude. The authors of this report are particularly alarmed by the 'derisory response' of rich countries when it comes to international adaptation finance (UNDP, 2007, p. 14). The report highlights the difference between the total resources pledged to the Least Developed Countries Fund established under the UNFCCC (US$279 million as of mid-2007, to be disbursed over several years) and the resources allocated to the Mose project, which aims to protect the city of Venice from sea level rise (US$3.8 billion over five years) (UNDP, 2007, p. 14). UNDP then calls for developed countries to mobilize the equivalent of 0.2% of their gross development product (GDP) for international adaptation finance, which is 'about one-tenth of what they currently spend on military programmes', noting that 'it is essential that (. . .) this international effort is additional to the agreed aid targets (. . .) and the broader aspirations to achieve an aid-to-GDP ratio of 0.7%' (UNDP, 2007, p. 194). This attention devoted to the scale of financial transfers only makes sense under a deontological attitude towards the evaluation of aid. Under such an attitude, the financial effort made by rich countries is valued as such.

The domination of a deontological attitude in the global debate on the allocation of adaptation finance is also reflected in the academic literature.

Roberts et al. (2017), for example, found that most of the peer-reviewed research published between 1997 and 2015 on this topic focuses on assessing the extent to which adaptation finance is distributed to the most vulnerable – rather than to where it can be most efficiently used. In the rest of this section, I first show how authoritative reports published by leading institutions actively involved in the global adaptation finance debate are also illustrative of this deontological attitude (Section 5.1). I then argue that the challenges associated with the monitoring of adaptation progress may explain the dominance of such an attitude towards the evaluation of adaptation finance (Section 5.2). I also review two prominent debates that are particularly illustrative of the tensions between a deontological attitude and a consequentialist attitude towards the evaluation of aid. The first of these debates opposes the mainstreaming of adaptation to the additionality of adaptation finance (Section 5.3). The second debate that I examine concerns the provision of loans to help developing countries adapt to climate change (Section 5.4).

5.1 Institutional Discourses on the Evaluation of Adaptation Finance

Let us briefly examine the extent to which recent authoritative reports on climate (adaptation) finance focus either on the scale and distribution of adaptation finance (which would reflect a deontological attitude) or on the impact of adaptation finance (reflecting a consequentialist attitude). Since 2014, the UNFCCC Standing Committee on Finance – composed of an equal number of representatives from developed and developing countries – has been publishing its flagship report entitled 'Biennial Assessment and Overview of Climate Finance Flows'. Its latest edition, published in November 2021, dedicates less than three pages to reviewing 'Emerging methodologies for measuring climate finance outcomes' (UNFCCC SCF, 2021a, pp. 45–8), mainly noting that 'There is currently no agreed standard on measuring the impact of (...) adaptation finance' (p. 45). This 216-page report also devotes a section to the 'Effectiveness of climate finance', with three subsections discussing 'access', 'ownership', and 'impact' of climate finance. While this section starts by mentioning that 'It is not just the volume of climate finance that is important but also how well that finance achieves its objectives' (p. 99), most of it does not discuss the impact of climate finance. In terms of access, the report notes that 'fair and equitable access to climate finance continues to be an important priority' (p. 99). The issue of 'ownership' is notably discussed through the prism of the alignment of climate finance with country needs. The half-page discussion on the impact of adaptation finance (p. 109) repeats that 'There is no singularly accepted impact metric for adaptation-focused climate finance' and that it is '(. . .) difficult to distinguish between good development and adaptation activities'. It adds that 'The timescale and frequency over which the multiple impacts of climate change will materialize further complicate the creation of common impact metrics for adaptation' (p. 109). I will come back to these challenges of assessing the impact of adaptation finance in Section 5.2 below.

The OECD's flagship annual report series on climate finance (published since 2015) focuses on the progress towards the US$100 billion mobilization goal. Recent editions contain information on the components (bilateral, multilateral, private, etc.), themes (adaptation, mitigation, and cross-cutting), instruments (grants, loans, etc.), sectors (energy, water and sanitation, etc.), and recipient regions (with a special focus on the allocation to Least Developed Countries and Small Island Developing States) of climate finance (see e.g., OECD, 2022). This annual report series makes almost no mention of effectiveness. The 2022 edition of the report reflects a timid change in focus as it dedicates for the first time a three-page section to 'Considerations relating to transparency, impacts and effectiveness' (OECD, 2022, pp. 44–6). The discussion on adaptation finance effectiveness is, however, limited to a couple of sentences, mainly highlighting various challenges and data gaps.

Oxfam's Climate Finance Shadow Reports (published biennially since 2016) similarly aim to provide an assessment of progress towards the US$100 billion goal. As highlighted in Section 1 of this Element, Oxfam's assessments considerably differ from the ones offered by the OECD (see also Roberts et al., 2021). However, Oxfam's reports similarly focus on the amount and allocation of climate finance. The latest edition of this report series nonetheless also discusses the need to expand resources to support locally led action and to support gender equality efforts, highlighting that 'Adaptation (. . .) action that is gender-blind risks being inefficient or ineffective' (see e.g., Oxfam, 2020, p. 23).

The 'Joint Report on Multilateral Development Banks' Climate Finance' annually published for more than ten years by leading multilateral development banks – including among others the African Development Bank, the Asian Development Bank, the European Bank for Reconstruction and Development, and the World Bank Group – do not include any information on adaptation outcomes (UNFCCC SCF, 2021a). It only provides information on adaptation finance flows, including their distribution across various regions (see e.g., MDB Joint Report, 2021).

To conclude this short review of reports published by leading organizations active in the adaptation finance debate, it is further enlightening to compare two series of documents published by the United Nations Environment Programme, respectively entitled 'The Emissions Gap Report' (annual publication since 2009) and 'The Adaptation Gap Report' (annual report since 2013). While the first series aims to assess the compatibility of the greenhouse gas mitigation pledges of the world's countries with the international commitment to limit the increase in global average temperature to 1.5 or 2°C compared to the pre-industrial period, the second series has long almost exclusively focused on the 'adaptation finance gap' by comparing adaptation needs in developing countries with the funding transferred to them by rich countries. The 2017 Adaptation Gap Report marked a broadening of the funding-centric approach of the first four Adaptation Gap Reports as it focused on trying to answer the question: 'What are the ways forward to assess progress towards the global goal on adaptation?' (UNEP, 2017, p. 3). While subsequent reports track gaps in terms of planning, finance and progress, considerable attention is still devoted to the 'widening' of the 'adaptation finance gap' as 'estimated adaptation costs in developing countries are five to ten times greater than current public adaptation finance flows [from developed countries]' (UNEP, 2021, p. 36).

The focus of UNEP Adaptation Gap Reports on financial resources needed by and transferred to developing countries is not surprising. The adaptation agenda remains intrinsically associated with or even assimilated to North-South financial transfers in international negotiations on climate change. The formulation of a 'global adaptation goal' in the Paris Agreement (UNFCCC, 2015, art. 7.1) was seen by some researchers as a crucial step to move beyond the funding-focused lens of the UNFCCC on adaptation (Magnan & Ribera, 2016; Lesnikowski et al., 2017). However, these hopes have only materialized to a limited extent since then (Magnan & Chalastani, 2019).

This lack of progress can be explained by the fact that negotiators from the Global North have always viewed such a global goal on adaptation with suspicion, fearing that it may primarily lead to new financial demands from developing countries. These financial demands are indeed obvious in the 'Submission on adaptation in the 2015 Agreement' made by Swaziland (2013) on behalf of the African Group. This submission states, for example, that 'the adaptation costs associated with the long-term [temperature] goal shall constitute the global adaptation goal' and that 'developed countries including those [listed] in Annex II [to the Convention] should provide support commensurate with science and the temperature goal' (Swaziland, 2013, p. 2).

Some developing country negotiators have also considered such a global goal on adaptation with caution, fearing that the receipt of adaptation finance could become conditional to the achievement of adaptation outcome targets that could potentially be imposed by the North. Many developing country negotiators are also very careful about the risk that the global goal on adaptation may distract climate negotiations on adaptation from its historic funding-focused lens.

For these countries, the priority remains to assess adaptation needs and to translate these needs into international funding requests (see Magnan & Chalastani, 2019).

5.2 The Key Issue of Uncertainty

A deontological attitude clearly dominates the evaluation of international adaptation finance. But is this attitude really chosen? As Naudet (2000) points out, aid can be explicitly considered legitimate in principle, without really questioning its effectiveness in producing desirable consequences. The discourses of many developing country negotiators and civil society representatives in international climate negotiations tend to show that the effectiveness of adaptation finance is indeed a secondary concern for these actors compared to the scale of financial resources transferred to developing countries. But the ultimate consequences of aid can also be ignored because they are too complex to assess (Naudet, 2000). This seems to be the position adopted by most actors active in the global adaptation finance debate, including bilateral and multilateral adaptation finance providers. These actors are indeed confronted with the complexity of evaluating the effectiveness of adaptation finance interventions in the long term.

The authors of the 2021 UNEP Adaptation Gap Report, for example, highlight '(. . .) the lack of knowledge about [the] outcomes of [adaptation projects] and the increasing concern over the way [they] are currently planned and implemented – and the implications this has for their effectiveness' (UNEP, 2021, p. 48). A recent evaluation of the Green Climate Fund's adaptation portfolio likewise found that the Fund 'currently has no systematic approach for assessing the depth of adaptation impacts' (GCF Independent Evaluation Unit, 2021, p. 11). The UNFCCC Standing Committee on Finance notes that 'It is difficult to measure the beneficiaries of an intervention to reduce the impact of a slow-onset event that will occur over many years, likely after the intervention has ended' (UNFCCC, 2021, p. 109).

Yet, most bilateral and multilateral aid actors seem to adopt a consequentialist attitude by assuming that reducing vulnerability to current climate conditions automatically reduces vulnerability to future climate change (Weikmans, 2015). However, measuring the effects of aid interventions on the level of adaptation to current climate conditions leads to 'low effectiveness' criteria that say little about the persistence of results over time. It is indeed often process indicators – rather than impact indicators – that are used to evaluate adaptation interventions, such as whether climate projections are considered in a given piece of legislation or the number of stormwater basins built (see Brooks et al., 2011; van

Gameren et al., 2014; Christiansen et al., 2018; Leiter et al., 2019; Pauw et al., 2020).

Assuming that the reduction of vulnerability to past or current climate conditions automatically leads to lower vulnerability to future climate stress allows aid actors to justify many of their current interventions and to perpetuate their traditional approaches of 'doing development' (Weikmans, 2017; see also Eriksen et al., 2021). However, it is not for sure that this assumption will hold in all cases. For example, interventions to develop a crop irrigation system in a specific area could be highly beneficial in the short to medium term but could lead to path dependency situations with potentially disastrous consequences (see Palutikof et al., 2013). Indeed, if water availability were to fall because of large-scale climate change, agricultural systems in the region could potentially experience a catastrophic collapse. The issue of adaptation to climate change undoubtedly invites us to (re)question the sustainability of current development trajectories (Weikmans, 2013; Eriksen et al., 2021).

5.3 Additionality of Funding and Mainstreaming of Adaptation into ODA

In this section, I want to illustrate how the deontological versus consequentialist analytical framework can shed light on the foundations of recurring debates linked to the evaluation of adaptation finance. I will focus on the contestations related to the mainstreaming of adaptation into ODA as this debate is particularly prominent in the academic literature (e.g., Ayers & Huq, 2009; Huq & Reid, 2009; Klein, 2010; Ayers & Abeysinghe, 2013; Ledant, 2016; Schipper et al., 2020). I will start by summarizing the controversies linked to the additionality of climate (adaptation) finance as they form the backdrop of the debate surrounding the mainstreaming of adaptation into ODA, that I will then explore.

The terms 'new and additional' have never been defined under the UNFCCC and their meaning has been the subject of intense contestation for more than thirty years (see e.g., Stadelmann et al., 2011; Weikmans & Roberts, 2019). For many civil society observers and developing country negotiators, the term 'new' generally refers to the fact that the funding in question should represent an increase over pre-existing climate finance flows. It is also sometimes understood as funding raised from 'new' sources such as a tax on financial transactions or on international air and maritime transport (Müller et al., 2010). However, no such source of adaptation finance has been implemented to date – except for the levy on carbon credits discussed in Section 1.2. The term 'additional' is often presented by these actors as aiming to ensure that financial resources raised to address climate change do not replace resources provided by rich countries to fund activities – such as building schools and hospitals – that have other socioeconomic development objectives (e.g., Oxfam, 2020; CARE, 2021b).

Most developing country representatives have persistently argued that funding should only be considered 'new and additional' if it exceeds the 0.7% target of national income that developed countries have long promised to devote to ODA (Khor, 2008). However, very few developed countries have reached this 0.7% target. Most adaptation finance flows therefore do not meet this definition of additionality. Some civil society observers have suggested that funds counted towards the US$100 billion goal should not also be counted towards the 0.7% aid target (Oxfam, 2020; CARE, 2021b). However, as highlighted in Section 1.2, almost all adaptation finance flows are counted by developed countries towards this 0.7% target. Acknowledging this, Oxfam (2020) proposes 'as a first step' that developed countries ensure that 'future increases of climate finance qualifying as ODA form part of an overall aid budget that is increasing at least at the same rate as climate finance' (Oxfam, 2020, p. 22).

While UNFCCC reporting guidelines do not contain any definition of the terms 'new and additional', they require each developed country to specify how they understand those terms (UNFCCC SCF, 2021a). Most developed countries provide a minimalist – not to say meaningless – definition, considering that 'new and additional' resources cover newly disbursed or committed finance in the reporting year (UNFCCC SCF, 2021a, p. 37). Ten developed countries have more stringent definitions, such as (for three of them) setting 2009 as the baseline year to determine which funding is 'new and additional'. Only two developed countries (i.e., Luxembourg and Sweden) consider 'new and additional' climate finance amounts as flows that exceeded the 0.7% target described above (Sweden, 2019, p. 128; Luxemburg, 2020, p. 238; UNFCCC SCF, 2021a, p. 37).

These contestations on the additionality of climate finance are the starting point of those related to the mainstreaming of adaptation into ODA. For at least 15 years, most development cooperation agencies have been paying increased attention to climate change adaptation considerations in the design and implementation of their aid activities (see OECD DAC, 2006; OECD, 2019). This 'adaptation mainstreaming' has long been advocated in both the academic and institutional literatures as a way to take advantage of the synergies or overlaps that exist at the operational level between activities aimed at promoting socioeconomic development and those aimed at reducing vulnerability to climate change (Ayers & Huq, 2009). This 'mainstreamed adaptation' is thus seen as allowing a more efficient use of available resources than 'stand-alone' adaptation projects that have adaptation as their core or only objective (Klein, 2010). In international climate negotiations, however, the mainstreaming of adaptation into ODA creates a dilemma. It is indeed difficult to assess the additionality of adaptation finance without clearly distinguishing it from development finance. The main concern expressed by many developing countries representatives is therefore that funding for adaptation could be 'diverted' from already limited ODA budgets, which would not increase accordingly. Let us summarize the main points of contention of this debate with the deontological versus consequentialist analytical framework previously presented.

A consequentialist perspective highlights the fact that using development aid channels makes sense from an operational point of view, as it allows the efficient integration of adaptation considerations into aid activities to help ensure the sustainability of their impact. From this perspective, the notion of additionality is problematic in that it would encourage the design of 'additional' adaptation projects. This perspective is very critical towards the channels established under the UNFCCC that tend to design stand-alone adaptation projects, with the many practical challenges that this implies. These dedicated funding channels are accused of promoting parallel planning processes, bypassing existing initiatives such as national development plans or poverty reduction strategies. This consequentialist perspective argues that adaptation poses a range of cross-cutting challenges to societies; designing it in a fragmented way therefore risks creating redundancies or leaving adaptation needs unfunded at the operational level.

By contrast, a deontological perspective insists that, for a variety of reasons, financial resources for adaptation should be additional to North-South financial transfers dedicated to other purposes. The effort of developed countries in this regard is seen as an objective in itself. This perspective stresses the importance of monitoring this financial effort given that the resources currently channelled to development aid and to adaptation finance are considered to be largely insufficient to address developing countries' needs. Most civil society observers and developing country representatives agree that implementing 'pure' adaptation projects makes little sense at the operational level (e.g., Singh & Bose, 2021), but they argue that the channels dedicated to funding adaptation established under the UNFCCC are the only ones that allow the additionality of funding to be truly assessed (e.g., Indian Ministry of Finance, 2015). These actors consider the mainstreaming of adaptation into ODA as a 'cheap' way for developed countries to fulfil their climate finance commitments. This perception is further reinforced by the tendency of some developed countries to 'inflate' their adaptation finance figures by reporting as 'adaptation finance' under the UNFCCC development assistance activities that have little to do with adaptation (see e.g., Junghans & Harmeling, 2012; Weikmans et al., 2017; Oxfam, 2020; CARE, 2021a).

This debate around the additionality of adaptation finance and the mainstreaming of adaptation into ODA is a dialogue of the deaf, as the arguments expressed by various stakeholders do not respond to each other. These arguments are situated at two different levels: the operationalization of adaptation in developing countries, on the one hand, and the mobilization of international financial support, on the other hand. It seems, however, clear that these contrasting positions respond at least partly to instrumental considerations, with developing countries' negotiators seeking to maximize the financial transfers to their countries and developed countries' representatives seeking to minimize the fiscal impact of their international financial commitments.

The tensions between the additionality of climate finance and the integration of climate considerations into ODA have not faded away in recent years. Breaking from more than two decades of environmental treaty-making, the Paris Agreement (UNFCCC, 2015) did not use the terms 'new and additional' when referring to climate finance (Roberts & Weikmans, 2015).[19] However, following intense pressure from developing countries, the words 'new and additional' reappeared three years later in the 'modalities, procedures and guidelines' of the Paris Agreement's enhanced transparency framework that detail – among other things – the information to be communicated to the UNFCCC Secretariat regarding climate finance provided to developing countries (UNFCCC, 2018c, Annex, para. 121). While developed country representatives try to elude the topic of additionality in climate negotiations, developing country negotiators and civil society observers systematically reiterate their demands that climate (adaptation) finance be 'new and additional' (see Weikmans & Roberts, 2018; Raman, 2021).

Since 2015, the tensions between the additionality of funding and the mainstreaming of climate considerations into ODA have been renewed by Article 2.1(c) of the Paris Agreement (UNFCCC, 2015) that aims at 'making finance flows consistent with a pathway towards low greenhouse gas emissions and climate-resilient development' (see e.g., Weikmans & Roberts, 2016; Affana et al., 2020; Zamarioli et al., 2021; Pauw et al., 2022). While this provision does not only concern ODA flows, it has revitalized interest in the integration of

---

[19] The Paris Agreement, however, mentioned that the provision of climate finance is to be made 'in continuation of developed countries' existing obligations under the Convention' (UNFCCC, 2015, art. 9.1). This provision implicitly refers to this 'new and additional' principle but developing country negotiators lost a battle by allowing these crucial words to be absent from the text of the Paris Agreement.

climate considerations into ODA (e.g., Larsen et al., 2018; OECD, 2019, 2021b). This 'Paris alignment' makes sense from an operational perspective as parts of ODA have been shown to conflict with mitigation and adaptation objectives (see e.g., OECD, 2019; Hårsmar & Hjelm, 2020; UK Independent Commission for Aid Impact, 2021).

However, from the point of view of a developing country climate negotiator primarily interested in securing increased financial transfers to the Global South, too much focus on this 'Paris Alignment' might be problematic. Indeed, as climate-related ODA forms the bulk of what developed countries report as 'climate finance' to the UNFCCC Secretariat, any rise in the amount of climate-related ODA could almost automatically lead to a rise in the figures that developed countries report as 'climate finance' to the UNFCCC, even if overall development finance flows to developing countries remain stable (or do not rise in the same proportion). We can therefore expect developing country climate negotiators to welcome with circumspection the 'Declaration on a new approach to align development co-operation with the goals of the Paris Agreement on Climate Change' published by OECD donor countries in October 2021 (OECD DAC, 2021a).

5.4 Grants or Loans

Should adaptation finance be exclusively provided in the form of grants? This question has always been highly controversial in international discussions on adaptation finance. It is also a particularly contentious issue for development aid in general (Cohen et al., 2006). Under a deontological perspective, the emphasis on the financial transfer – which is 'owed' to developing countries – and the relatively low importance devoted to the principle of cost-effectiveness mean that aid is essentially conceptualized as grants (see Jacquet & Naudet, 2006, pp. 69–70). By contrast, loans are inherently consequentialist: Adaptation projects financed by loans have to be designed in a profitable way so that the borrowed capital can be repaid. Tenants of a consequentialist perspective (mainly developed countries and multilateral development institutions) stress the multiplying effect that loans can have as they mobilize more co-finance and because repaid loans can be re-invested in new climate projects (Pauw et al., 2022).

The official position of the G77 and China – a negotiating bloc of more than 130 developing countries – is that financing for adaptation should be grant-based (see e.g., G77 & China, 2015). Many global charities and environmental NGOs share a similar point of view. Various arguments are put forward in support of such a position. There is first the idea that developing countries should not be forced to pay twice, both for the damage inflicted by polluting countries through their historical and current responsibility for climate change and for new debts incurred to face climate impacts. For Oxfam, 'The world's poorest countries and communities should not be forced to take out loans to protect themselves from the excess carbon emissions of rich countries' (Oxfam, 2020, p. 3). A related argument is that the Global North owes a 'climate debt' to the Global South and that adaptation finance constitutes the payment of this debt (see Khan et al., 2020). Another often-made argument is that while loans may be adequate to finance mitigation activities, '(. . .) for example where cheap capital is needed to cover high start-up costs of renewable energy projects, which will be paid back over time', adaptation finance '(. . .) should always be provided in the form of grants' (Oxfam, 2012, p. 6).

Some analysts have also criticized the use of loans for climate finance on the grounds that they could increase the debt burden of vulnerable countries (Müller & Winkler, 2008; Seballos & Kreft, 2011). This last argument has been particularly prominent since the COVID-19 outbreak as the pandemic has deeply altered the fiscal and debt situation of many developing countries, especially the poorest ones (Bhattacharya et al., 2020). As of December 2021, about 60% of low-income countries were at high risk or already in debt distress, despite significant relief measures taken over the previous months (Georgieva & Pazarbasioglu, 2021). Many middle-income countries are also under deep fiscal pressure (Bhattacharya et al., 2020). This has led some civil society organizations to call for new debt cancellations, highlighting that 'Lower income countries spend five times more on debt payments than for dealing with climate change' (Jubilee Debt Campaign, 2021, p. 1). The current debt situation of many poor countries has also renewed interest in 'debt-for-climate swap' (e.g., Essers et al., 2021; Thomas & Theokritoff, 2021; earlier proposals include Fenton et al., 2014), an instrument through which a debtor government agrees to use the reduced amount of (the service of) its debt to implement climate actions.

Neither the Copenhagen Accord (UNFCCC, 2009), nor the Cancun Agreements (UNFCCC, 2010) mentions the extent to which the US$100 billion mobilization goal should take the form of grants or loans. No decision text has provided more clarity on this issue since then. As with the other parameters of the climate finance pledges, significant discretion has therefore been left to developed countries on how they implement their financial commitments. Available OECD data show that 62% of public adaptation finance were provided in the form of loans in 2016–2020 (OECD, 2022). Despite the official position of the G77 and China in international climate negotiations, many developing countries have therefore accepted loans to finance adaptation activities.[20] For Oxfam, 'The excessive use of loans and the provision of non-concessional finance in the name of climate assistance is an overlooked scandal' (Oxfam, 2020, p. 3). It is, however, important to note that developed countries have diverging practices in this regard as some of them only provide their climate finance in the form of grants (see Section 1.2). By contrast, the main multilateral development banks provide a significant proportion of their concessional adaptation finance in the form of loans (76% in 2017–2018) (UNFCCC SCF, 2021a, p. 93).

Regarding the multilateral climate funds established under the UNFCCC, the Convention text (UNFCCC, 1992, art. 11.1) explicitly states that its financial mechanism can provide financial resources 'on a grant or concessional basis', which therefore comprises concessional loans. However, it is significant to note that none of the three so-called 'Marrakech Funds' (i.e., the Least Developed Countries Fund, the Special Climate Change Fund, and the Adaptation Fund) provides loans. By contrast, the Green Climate Fund does provide grants and loans for adaptation, not without attracting criticisms (e.g., Huq, 2015).

The World Bank's Pilot Program for Climate Resilience (PPCR) – the biggest multilateral adaptation fund established outside the UNFCCC – similarly attracted considerable criticism from civil society observers for providing loans to developing countries to help them adapt to the effects of climate change (Ayers & Huq, 2009; Seballos & Kreft, 2011). Faced with these criticisms, the World Bank highlighted the fact that the loans offered to countries selected for the pilot phase of the PPCR were 'optional'. This emphasis on the optional nature of the proposed loans is important to highlight as it illustrates one more time the fact that the adaptation finance agenda tends to be driven by a deontological perspective towards the evaluation of aid. Importantly, ActionAid (2009, p. 24) observed that 'while the World Bank says that loans are "optional," in reality many countries will not have the choice to refuse these loans because they are in desperate need of adaptation finance'.

Another crucial dimension of the grants versus loans debate concerns how loans are counted as part of developed countries' climate finance commitments under the UNFCCC. Except for Germany, all developed countries that provide loans report grants and loans in the same way, by recording the flows of cash that are granted and the face value of loans that are provided to developing countries (Weikmans & Roberts, 2019). A grant of US$10 million therefore appears equal to a loan of US$10 million in the climate finance figures reported to the

---

[20] This disconnection between on the one hand official positions expressed within the UNFCCC negotiations and on the other hand practices of individual countries can also be illustrated by the fact that (to the best of my knowledge) no developing country has refused financial resources for adaptation on the basis that they were not 'new and additional'.

UNFCCC by most developed countries. In addition, no distinction is made between concessional and non-concessional loans. What is more, loan repayments are not deducted from reported figures (Weikmans & Roberts, 2019).

In a clearly deontological perspective, developing country negotiators (Indian Ministry of Finance, 2015), NGO representatives (Oxfam, 2020; CARE, 2021a), and various other observers (Roberts et al., 2021) have repeatedly criticized these accounting practices on the ground that they do not reflect the actual financial efforts made by developed countries. Dissensions exist between rich countries on this issue, but they have always resisted calls for strict accounting rules under the UNFCCC that would require them to report their loans in 'grant equivalents' (Weikmans & Roberts, 2019). Such reporting would allow a better assessment of developed countries' respective financial efforts and would make it possible to compare the performance of developed countries in terms of providing financial support to developing countries.

In 2018, developed countries finally conceded to report the 'grant-equivalent value' of financial support provided and mobilized under the Paris Agreement, but this will only happen 'on a voluntary basis' and not before 2024 (UNFCCC, 2018c, Annex, paras. 123–125), which has proved deeply unsatisfying to many observers (Weikmans et al., 2020a). The lack of progress on reporting climate finance in grant equivalents under the UNFCCC is likely due to political rather than technical reasons, as a grant equivalent system became the OECD standard for measuring ODA in 2019, following a decision taken in 2014 (see OECD DAC, 2021b). Under the UNFCCC, this debate is politically complicated by the fact that transitioning to a grant equivalent system would mechanically push developed countries further away from reaching the 'totemic' US$100 billion goal. In any case, the importance that this debate on grant equivalent reporting now occupies clearly reflects a deontological perspective towards the evaluation of climate (adaptation) finance.

5.5 Conclusion

In this section, I have highlighted the specific attitude towards the evaluation of aid that accompanies the international financial efforts in favour of adaptation in developing countries. To do so, I used the classic opposition in theories of justice between a consequentialist attitude and a deontological attitude, as conceptualized by several development aid scholars. I have shown the extent to which questions related to the scale of international adaptation finance and its allocation to the most vulnerable are central to international scientific and political debates on adaptation. The importance given to them reflects an ethical attitude towards the evaluation of aid in which financial transfers are legitimate in themselves, regardless of their ultimate consequences for climate change adaptation.

This attitude towards evaluation is undoubtedly 'chosen' by some actors, such as developing country negotiators and representatives of international development charities. The posture of traditional bilateral and multilateral donors is more precarious, as they are deeply involved in a consequentialist attitude towards the evaluation of aid in general. Most of them implicitly or explicitly assume that their interventions that reduce vulnerability to current climate conditions (an impact that can be measured) automatically reduce vulnerability to future climate change (an impact that is too complex to evaluate). However, it is unlikely that this assumption will hold true in all cases.

By allowing for an intermediate attitude between a deontological and a consequentialist attitude, this assumption is nevertheless effective in terms of financial mobilization. Indeed, a strict deontological attitude is difficult to maintain for donors as they might lose their motivation to provide financial resources if they are led to support activities that they consider useless or even harmful (Opeskin, 1996). As Naudet puts it: 'Do we have a duty to intervene when we know that someone is misusing our resources?' (Naudet, 2006, p. 163, my translation). Moreover, a strongly consequentialist attitude rarely goes with abundant resources devoted to aid: Who would want to finance a public policy whose limits and harmful effects are constantly being highlighted?

It is also significant to note that discourses on international adaptation finance generally avoid the question of 'absorptive capacity' – often defined as 'the ability to use additional aid without pronounced inefficiency of public spending and without induced adverse effects' (Bourguignon & Sundberg, 2007, p. 640). This is not surprising as this question is meaningless in a deontological attitude towards the evaluation of aid; however, it is crucial in a consequentialist attitude since the achievement of persisting effects fundamentally depends on the capacity of recipient countries to absorb aid.

6 General Conclusion

All international donors, whether bilateral, regional, or multilateral, have now explicitly incorporated – albeit to varying degrees – climate change adaptation considerations into their activities (OECD, 2019, 2021b). While the rapid emergence of adaptation on the international development agenda is unquestionably remarkable, it also remains precarious in some respects. After all, it was only in 2010 that the OECD explicitly started to monitor the mainstreaming of adaptation considerations into development cooperation activities (see Weikmans et al., 2017). Three main points can be further highlighted to conclude this Element and to suggest directions for future research.

6.1 Financial Mobilization

The normative oppositions examined in the previous sections help explain the significant financial mobilization of developed countries towards adaptation in the Global South – or at least the scale of their financial promises in this regard. Indeed, for each of the four sets of questions examined in this Element, dominant discourses on adaptation finance are mainly situated in the normative dimensions that are associated with a maximum commitment to aid (see shaded cells in Table 5).

Whether they adopt an outcome or a contextual interpretation of vulnerability, dominant assessments of the causes of high levels of climate risk faced by developing countries give a central place to climate stresses (see Section 2). These external factors are associated with a high duty of intervention on the part of developed countries as their responsibility for climate change is often highlighted. Moreover, the discourses of many actors combine moral obligations of distributive and corrective justice (see Section 3). The redistributive claims often made by these actors are then reinforced by corrective concerns, that sometimes explicitly encompass compensations for the consequences of climate change on the hardest hit countries.

These discourses, fully embedded in a conception of aid as a right, push for the allocation of financial resources to those countries that need it the most (see Section 4). They also often call for the absolute respect for the beneficiaries' choices in terms of the use of transferred resources. Any form of conditionality is viewed with a great deal of suspicion, even resentment. Moreover, the uncertainties linked to the ultimate consequences of adaptation interventions lead to a mixed attitude towards the question of evaluation (Section 5). The limits and shortcomings of donors' adaptation interventions are not often highlighted (exceptions exist, see e.g., Eriksen et al., 2021). In fact, there seems to be some form of consensus on the effectiveness of aid interventions in the area of adaptation, so that this effectiveness is hardly questioned. The central criteria for assessing adaptation finance are the scale of the amounts mobilized by developed countries and their distribution to the most vulnerable developing countries. All these dimensions are conducive to a very high financial mobilization towards developing countries.

6.2 Which Vision of Aid?

The sections of this Element have illustrated how the discourses on adaptation finance of many developing country negotiators, environmental NGOs,

Table 5 Normative dimensions of aid

Responsibility for climate risk

Causes	*External causes*		*Internal causes*
	Endogenous to developed countries	*Exogenous to developed countries*	
Developed countries' duty to act	High	Medium	Low

Moral duty

	Distributive justice	*Corrective justice*
Justification of aid	Responding to an unfair distribution of resources	Repairing injustices that are precisely identified and located in time
Purpose of aid	No fixed purpose: continuous transfers of resources between those who have more and those who have less than their 'fair share'	Restoration of the situation of the subject of the injustice as if it had never happened; may lead to compensation
Function of aid	Redistribution	Reparation

Allocation

	Liberal perspective	*Perfectionist perspective*
Vision	Aid as a right	Aid as an incentive
Allocation	Automatic, according to the needs of beneficiaries	According to a contract between the donor and the beneficiary
Use of financial resources	Free	Restricted to specific uses (targeted aid); Free use but other commitments (conditional aid)

Evaluation

	Deontological attitude	*Consequentialist attitude*
Evaluation criteria	Donor countries' financial effort; Fairness of resource allocation	Efficiency in producing results; Sustainable, persistent impact
Underlying logic	Aid as a financial transfer	Aid as an investment

Note: The shaded cells are those associated with dominant discourses on international adaptation finance.

development charities, academics, and international bureaucrats renew a specific vision of aid, that of an aid intended to respond to international injustices and to fuel a regular transfer of resources between rich and poor countries. This vision of aid was dominant in the 1970s during the debates on the New International Economic Order (NIEO) (Jacquet & Naudet, 2006; Naudet et al., 2007). Further research could compare the origins, claims, achievements, and failures of the NIEO with those related to adaptation finance. There is no doubt that such an analysis would reveal many differences, given that the world has undergone profound changes over the past fifty years. However, some similarities could probably be highlighted.

For example, in the 1970s, dominant explanations of the poverty of then so-called Third World countries revolved around external causes such as unequal trade rules, legacies of colonization, failures of the international monetary system and deregulation of transnational corporations (Naudet, 2006; Zacharie, 2013; Rothstein, 2015). The emphasis currently placed by dominant discourses on external factors to explain the high levels of climate risk faced by developing countries is partly similar – even if the external factors are different that the ones highlighted in the context of the NIEO. Other similarities include strong demands from developing countries' representatives for a significant redistribution of global wealth and for greater control by these countries over international institutions.

It may also be possible to identify similarities between the modesty of the realizations associated with the NIEO (see e.g., Clerc, 2009) and the limited concretization of the demands expressed by developing country and civil society representatives on adaptation finance. Some of these demands have been successfully translated in tangible realizations. The Adaptation Fund probably represents the most accomplished of these realizations, with its innovative source of funding based on a form of international taxation, its board dominated by developing country representatives, and the possibility for these countries to directly access the resources of the Fund.

It remains, however, to be seen whether these achievements – widely celebrated by developing country negotiators and various civil society representatives – will go beyond the status of mere symbolic victories. I must again stress the low level of funding that has been channelled to date through the funds established under the UNFCCC – that a long-time observer of international climate negotiations describes as 'placebo funds' (Müller, 2011, p. 5). Recent pledges made to the Green Climate Fund (GCF, 2022) roughly mean that it could annually devote US$1 billion to adaptation in developing countries over the next coming years. While significant, this amount represents a limited portion of overall adaptation finance flows and a fraction of developing countries' needs.

The claims associated with the NIEO were weakened by discourses that highlighted the importance of internal causes in the persistent poverty of developing countries. The demands for financial transfers for adaptation could similarly be weakened if dominant assessments were to further qualify the role played by climate change in the high levels of climate risks faced by developing countries. For example, in December 2021, the findings of the *World Weather Attribution initiative* – an international team of climate scientists – highlighted poverty, poor infrastructure and dependence on rain-fed agriculture as the main factors of the food crisis that was happening in Southern Madagascar, thereby contradicting claims made a couple of days before by the World Food Programme according to which climate change was the main driver of food insecurity in the region (see Tandon, 2021). Conversely, it is likely that the occurrence in the Global South of particularly extreme or even unprecedented hydrometeorological events leading to large-scale disasters such as those that hit Pakistan in August 2022 could have a strong influence on public opinions in developed countries, pushing their governments to accept some of the financial demands made by developing countries, international development charities and environmental NGOs. Yet all these hypotheses require further empirical scrutiny.

Discourses on loss and damage finance – an issue that has recently attracted growing attention under the UNFCCC – could also be analysed with the normative lenses used in this Element. Voices from developing countries and civil society groups have been pushing for years for loss and damage to be fully recognized as a third pillar of climate policy, beyond mitigation and adaptation (see e.g., Gewirtzman et al., 2018; Broberg & Romera, 2021). The discourses of these actors tend to highlight climate change as the main determinant of increasing climate-related impacts happening in the Global South and to stress the historical responsibility of developed countries in climate change (e.g., Sharma-Khushal et al., 2022, p. 6). As I have detailed throughout this Element, these positions put a very high duty on developed countries to help developing nations. At COP26 in Glasgow in 2021, the G77 and China called for the establishment of a dedicated loss and damage finance facility that would be funded by developed countries. Unsurprisingly, developed country representatives opposed such a demand; they nonetheless accepted the setting up of a three-year 'Glasgow Dialogue' that could eventually lead to the creation of some kind of new funding facility (Liao et al., 2022). Such a facility would represent an important symbolic gain for developing countries, but based on past and current experience, it is far from assured that developed countries would devote significant resources to it – especially if 'developing' countries such as China, Saudi Arabia, or Singapore do not chip in. Nonetheless, the potential creation of such a facility is already renewing some of the debates that I have reviewed in this Element, for example, on the 'newness and additionality' of funding or on the importance of public and grant-based financial flows to poor countries (see e.g., Sharma-Khushal et al., 2022, pp. 18–19).

6.3 Beyond International Adaptation Finance

In international climate negotiations, developed countries' support towards adaptation in developing countries remains mainly conceptualized as a transfer of financial resources. This dominant framing reaffirms the role of aid as a permanent mechanism for managing North-South relations. However, it is clearly over-simplistic in view of the interferences and synergies between aid and various other public policies of rich countries.

Developed countries' migration policies, the fight against illicit financial flows, direct and indirect export subsidies for agricultural products from rich countries: These are just some of the policy issues that ultimately impact poor countries' adaptation to climate change. Developed countries' greenhouse gas emission reduction policies constitute other examples. Even if the relative share of developed countries in global emissions is shrinking, mitigation efforts in the Global North are crucial to limit the scale of climate impacts that developing countries will have to face. The nature of the mitigation policies that are implemented is also crucial: It has been well documented (see e.g., FAO, 2003) that the boom in first-generation biofuels (produced from food crop products) supported by rich countries' public policies had an impact on the surge in global food prices in 2008 and 2011–2012, increasing the vulnerability of poor populations to climate-related events (by negatively affecting their food security).

Reflecting the dominant framing of international negotiations under the UNFCCC, this Element has mainly focused on North-South financial transfers for adaptation. Future research and policy efforts should pay more attention to the issue of policy coherence, by considering the impact that rich countries' other public policies can have on developing countries' adaptation to climate change.

References

ActionAid (2009). *Equitable adaptation finance.* www.actionaidusa.org/assets/
pdfs/climate_change/equitable_adaptation_finance.pdf.

Adaptation Fund (2011). *The Adaptation Fund project review process: Lessons
learned.* www.adaptation-fund.org/wp-content/uploads/2015/01/AFB
.PPRC_.7.3%20Lessons%20learned%20on%20the%20AF%20Project%
20Review%20Process.pdf.

Adaptation Fund (2013). *Instructions for preparing a request for project or
programme funding from the Adaptation Fund.* www.adaptation-fund.org/
wp-content/uploads/2015/03/OPG-ANNEX-4-2-Instructions-Nov2013.pdf.

Adaptation Fund (2017). *Instructions for preparing a request for project or
programme funding from the Adaptation Fund.* www.adaptation-fund.org/
wp-content/uploads/2021/05/Instructions-for-Preparing-a-Request-for-
ProjectProgramme-Funding_Oct-2017.pdf.

Adaptation Fund (2021a). *Adaptation Fund doubles the amount of funding
countries can access.* www.adaptation-fund.org/adaptation-fund-doubles-
the-amount-of-funding-countries-can-access-enhancing-access-to-climate-
finance-among-most-vulnerable/.

Adaptation Fund (2021b). *Operational policies and guidelines for parties to
access resources from the Adaptation Fund.* www.adaptation-fund.org/wp-
content/uploads/2017/08/OPG-amended-in-October-2021_adopted-clean
.pdf.

Adaptation Fund (2021c). *Press release: Adaptation Fund raises record US$
356 million in new pledges at COP26 for its concrete actions to most
vulnerable.* www.adaptation-fund.org/wp-content/uploads/2021/11/Press-
Release_111121_Adaptation-Fund-Raises-Record-US-356-Million-in-New-
Pledges-at-COP26-for-its-Concrete-Actions-to-Most-Vulnerable-3.pdf.

Adger, W. N., & Barnett, J. (2009). Four reasons for concern about adaptation to
climate change. *Environment and Planning A, 41*(12), 2800–5.

Affana, J. P. B., Bartosch, S., Ryfisch, D., Sidner, L., & Fekete, H. (2020).
*Climate finance: Accelerating the transition to carbon neutrality and climate
resilience.* Germanwatch, NewClimate Institute, and World Resources
Institute. https://germanwatch.org/sites/default/files/Memo3%20-%
20Climate%20Finance.%20MDB%20Paris%20alignment.pdf.

Ayers, J. (2011). Resolving the adaptation paradox: Exploring the potential for
deliberative adaptation policy-making in Bangladesh. *Global Environmental
Politics, 11*(1), 62–88.

Ayers, J., & Abeysinghe, A. (2013). International aid and adaptation to climate change. In Falkner, R. (Ed.). *The handbook of global climate and environment policy.* John Wiley, pp. 486–507.

Ayers, J., & Dodman, D. (2010). Climate change adaptation and development I: The state of the debate. *Progress in Development Studies, 10*(2), 161–8.

Ayers, J., & Huq, S. (2009). Supporting adaptation to climate change: What role for official development assistance? *Development Policy Review, 27,* 675–92.

Baer, P. (2006). Adaptation: Who pays whom? In Adger, W. N., Paavola, J., Huq, S., & Mace, M. J. (Eds.). *Fairness in adaptation to climate change.* MIT Press, pp. 131–53.

Barr, R., Fankhauser, S., & Hamilton, K. (2010). Adaptation investments: A resource allocation framework. *Mitigation and Adaptation Strategies for Global Change, 15,* 843–58.

Barrett, S. (2013). Local level climate justice? Adaptation finance and vulnerability reduction. *Global Environmental Change, 23*(6), 1819–29.

Beitz, C. R. (2000). Rawls's law of peoples. *Ethics, 110*(4), 669–96.

Betzold, C., & Weiler, F. (2017). Allocation of aid for adaptation to climate change: Do vulnerable countries receive more support? *International Environmental Agreements: Politics, Law and Economics, 17*(1), 17–36.

Betzold, C., & Weiler, F. (2018). *Development aid and adaptation to climate change in developing countries.* Springer.

Betzold, C., Castro, P., & Weiler, F. (2012). AOSIS in the UNFCCC negotiations: From unity to fragmentation? *Climate Policy, 12*(5), 591–613.

Bhattacharya, A., Calland, R., Averchenkova, A. et al. (2020). *Delivering on the $100 billion climate finance commitment and transforming climate finance.* Independent Expert Group on Climate Finance. www.un.org/sites/un2.un .org/files/100_billion_climate_finance_report.pdf.

Bodle, R., & Noens, V. (2018). Climate finance: Too much on detail, too little on the big picture? *Carbon & Climate Law Review, 12*(3), 248–57.

Bourguignon, F., & Sundberg, M. (2007). Absorptive capacity and achieving the MDGs. In Mavrotas, G., & Shorrocks, A. (Eds.). *Advancing development.* Palgrave Macmillan, pp. 640–63.

Broberg, M., & Romera, B. M. (Eds.). (2021). *The third pillar of international climate change policy: On 'loss and damage'after the Paris Agreement.* Routledge.

Brooks, N., Fisher, S., Rai, N. et al. (2011). *Tracking adaptation and measuring development: A step-by-step guide.* International Institute for Environment and Development. https://pubs.iied.org/sites/default/files/pdfs/migrate/ 10100IIED.pdf.

Brown, S. (2020). The rise and fall of the aid effectiveness norm. *The European Journal of Development Research, 32*(4), 1230–48.

CARE (2021a). *Climate adaptation finance: Fact or fiction?* CARE Denmark and CARE Netherlands. https://careclimatechange.org/wp-content/uploads/2021/01/CARE_Synthesis-report_Final_April-2021.pdf.

CARE (2021b). *New and additional climate finance contributed in 2018.* CARE International UK. https://reliefweb.int/sites/reliefweb.int/files/resources/CIUK_New_and_additional_climate_finance_contributed_in_2018.pdf.

Carmin, J., Tierney, K., Chu, E. et al. (2015). Adaptation to climate change. In Dunlap, R. E., & Brule, R. J. (Eds.). *Climate change and society: Sociological perspectives.* Oxford University Press, pp. 164–98.

Carr, S., McAuliffe, E., & MacLachlan, M. (1998). *Psychology of aid.* Routledge.

Chapagain, D., Baarsch, F., Schaeffer, M., & D'haen, S. (2020). Climate change adaptation costs in developing countries: Insights from existing estimates. *Climate and Development, 12*(10), 934–42.

Charnoz, O., & Severino, J.-M. (2015). *L'aide publique au développement.* Éditions La Découverte.

Chatterjee, D. K. (2004). *The ethics of assistance: Morality and the distant needy.* Cambridge University Press.

Christiansen, L., Martinez, G., & Naswa, P. (Eds.). (2018). *Adaptation metrics: Perspectives on measuring, aggregating and comparing adaptation results.* UNEP DTU Partnership. https://resilientcities2018.iclei.org/wp-content/uploads/UDP_Perspectives-Adaptation-Metrics-WEB.pdf.

Ciplet, D., & Roberts, J. T. (2017). Climate change and the transition to neoliberal environmental governance. *Global Environmental Change, 46,* 148–56.

Ciplet, D., Roberts, J. T., & Khan, M. (2013). The politics of international climate adaptation funding: Justice and divisions in the greenhouse. *Global Environmental Politics, 13,* 49–68.

Ciplet, D., Roberts, J. T., & Khan, M. R. (2015). *Power in a warming world.* MIT Press.

Ciplet, D., Adams, K. M., Weikmans, R., & Roberts, J. T. (2018). The transformative capability of transparency in global environmental governance. *Global Environmental Politics, 18*(3), 130–50.

Clarke, J. N. (1999). Ethics and humanitarian intervention. *Global Society, 13*(4), 489–510.

Clerc, D. (2009). *L'économie de A à Z.* Alternatives Economiques.

Climate Watch (2022). *GHG emissions.* www.climatewatchdata.org/ghg-emissions.

Cohen, D., Jacquet, P., & Reisen, H. (2006). Beyond 'grants versus loans': How to use debt for development. *Proceedings of the 3rd AFD-EUDN Conference*, pp. 163–90.

Colenbrander, S., Pettinotti, L., & Cao, Y. (2022). *A fair share of climate finance? An appraisal of past performance, future pledges and prospective contributors*. Overseas Development Institute. https://cdn.odi.org/media/documents/A_fair_share_of_climate_finance.pdf.

Council of the European Union (2020). *Council conclusions on climate diplomacy*. https://data.consilium.europa.cu/doc/document/ST-5033-2020-INIT/en/pdf.

de Guio, S., & Rencki, J. (2011). *Le Fonds d'adaptation, laboratoire du financement du changement climatique*. Working Paper 10/11. IDDRI/Sciences Po.

Dellink, R., Den Elzen, M., Aiking, H. et al. (2009). Sharing the burden of financing adaptation to climate change. *Global Environmental Change*, *19*(4), 411–21.

Dessai, S., Hulme, M., Lempert, R., & Pielke Jr, R. (2009). Do we need better predictions to adapt to a changing climate? *Eos, Transactions American Geophysical Union*, *90*(13), 111–12.

Doshi, D., & Garschagen, M. (2020). Understanding adaptation finance allocation: Which factors enable or constrain vulnerable countries to access funding? *Sustainability*, *12*(4308), 1–18.

Duus-Otterström, G. (2016). Allocating climate adaptation finance: Examining three ethical arguments for recipient control. *International Environmental Agreements: Politics, Law and Economics*, *16*(5), 655–70.

Elbehri, A., Genest, A., & Burfisher, M. (2011). *Global action on climate change in agriculture*. Food and Agriculture Organization of the United Nations.

Eriksen, S., Schipper, E. L. F., Scoville-Simonds, M. et al. (2021). Adaptation interventions and their effect on vulnerability in developing countries: Help, hindrance or irrelevance? *World Development*, *141*, 105383.

Essers, D., Cassimon, D., & Prowse, M. (2021). Debt-for-climate swaps: Killing two birds with one stone? *Global Environmental Change*, *71*, 102407.

Fair and Effective Climate Finance (2010). *An assessment of finance in global climate negotiations*. Third World Network. www.twn.my/title2/climate/pdf/fair_and_effective_climate_finance/Finance%20Assessment_En_Final.pdf.

Falzon, D. (2021). Expertise and exclusivity in adaptation decision-making. *Current Opinion in Environmental Sustainability*, *51*, 95–100.

Fankhauser, S. (2010). The costs of adaptation. *Wiley Interdisciplinary Reviews: Climate Change*, *1*, 23–30.

FAO (2003). *Biofuels and food security.* Food and Agriculture Organization of the United Nations. www.fao.org/publications/card/en/c/54b0ec34-18ea-500d-8172-428a3b3cf565.

Farand, C. (2021). Row erupts at Green Climate Fund over who defines climate adaptation. *Climate Home News*, 2 July. www.climatechangenews.com/2021/07/02/row-erupts-green-climate-fund-defines-climate-adaptation/.

Feindouno, S., Guillaumont, P., & Simonet, C. (2020). The physical vulnerability to climate change index: An index to be used for international policy. *Ecological Economics, 176*, 106752.

Fenton, A., Wright, H., Afionis, S., Paavola, J., & Huq, S. (2014). Debt relief and financing climate change action. *Nature Climate Change, 4*(8), 650–3.

Ford, J. D., Pearce, T., McDowell, G. et al. (2018). Vulnerability and its discontents: The past, present, and future of climate change vulnerability research. *Climatic Change, 151*(2), 189–203.

Forsyth, T. (2013). Community-based adaptation: a review of past and future challenges. *Wiley Interdisciplinary Reviews: Climate Change, 4*(5), 439–446.

Friedman, L., & Samuelsohn, D. (2009). Hillary Clinton pledges $100B for developing countries. *The New York Times*, 17 December. https://archive.nytimes.com/www.nytimes.com/cwire/2009/12/17/17climatewire-hillary-clinton-pledges-100b-for-developing-96794.html.

Füssel, H. M. (2007). Vulnerability: A generally applicable conceptual framework for climate change research. *Global Environmental Change, 17*(2), 155–67.

Füssel, H. M., Hallegatte, S., & Reder, M. (2012). International adaptation funding. In Eden-Hofer, O., Wallacher, J., Lotze-Campen, H. et al. (Eds.). *Climate change, justice and sustainability: Linking climate and development policy.* Springer Netherlands, pp. 311–30.

G7 (2021). *Carbis Bay G7 summit Communiqué.* https://assets.publishing.service.gov.uk/government/uploads/system/uploads/attachment_data/file/1001128/Carbis_Bay_G7_Summit_Communique__PDF__430KB__25_pages_.pdf.

G77, & China (2015). *G77 and China proposed texts to the note by the co-chairs (non-paper), dated 5 October 2015 article 6 (finance).* https://unfccc.int/sites/default/files/g77_and_china_proposed_texts_to_the_note_by_the_co.pdf.

Garschagen, M., & Doshi, D. (2022). Does funds-based adaptation finance reach the most vulnerable countries? *Global Environmental Change, 73*, 102450.

GCF (2011). *Governing instrument for the Green Climate Fund.* Green Climate Fund. www.greenclimate.fund/sites/default/files/document/governing-instrument.pdf.

GCF (2021). *Policy on incremental cost and full cost methodologies*. Green Climate Fund. www.greenclimate.fund/sites/default/files/document/gcf-b29-infl0.pdf.

GCF (2022). *Status of pledges and contributions (status date: 31 July 2022)*. Green Climate Fund. www.greenclimate.fund/sites/default/files/document/status-pledges-july-31-2022.pdf.

GCF Independent Evaluation Unit (2021). *Final report on the independent evaluation of the adaptation portfolio and approach of the Green Climate Fund*. Green Climate Fund's Independent Evaluation Unit. https://ieu.green climate.fund/document/independent-evaluation-adaptation-portfolio-and-approach-green-climate-fund.

GEF (2012). *Clarification on the concept of additional costs of adaptation to climate change*. Global Environment Facility. www.thegef.org/sites/default/files/council-meeting-documents/Clarification_on_Additional_Cost_8_May.pdf.

GEF (2018). *Policy & guidelines on system for transparent allocation of resources (STAR)*. Global Environment Facility. www.thegef.org/sites/default/files/documents/STAR_Policy_Guidelines.pdf.

Georgieva, K., & Pazarbasioglu, C. (2021). The G20 common framework for debt treatments must be stepped up. *IMF Blog*, 2 December. https://blogs.imf.org/2021/12/02/the-g20-common-framework-for-debt-treatments-must-be-stepped-up/.

Gewirtzman, J., Natson, S., Richards, J. A. et al. (2018). Financing loss and damage: Reviewing options under the Warsaw International Mechanism. *Climate Policy*, *18*(8), 1076–86.

Grasso, M. (2010). An ethical approach to climate adaptation finance. *Global Environmental Change*, *20*(1), 74–81.

Gupta, J. (2009). Climate change and development cooperation: Trends and questions. *Current Opinion in Environmental Sustainability*, *1*(2), 207–13.

Hallegatte, S. (2008). *A note on including climate change adaptation in an international scheme*. Working Paper 18/08. IDDRI/Sciences Po. www.iddri.org/en/node/21303.

Hallegatte, S., Brandon, C., Damania, R. et al. (2018). *The economics of (and obstacles to) aligning development and climate change adaptation*. World Bank. https://gca.org/wp-content/uploads/2018/10/18_WP_GCA_Economics_1001_final.pdf.

Harmeling, S., & Kaloga, A. O. (2011). Understanding the political economy of the Adaptation Fund. *IDS Bulletin*, *42*(3), 23–32.

Hårsmar, M., & Hjelm, L. (2020). *Alignment of Sweden's multilateral aid with the Paris Agreement on climate change*. EBA Working Paper Series. Working

Paper November 2020 https://eba.se/wp-content/uploads/2020/11/WP-2020_11_H%C3%A5rsmar-4.pdf.

Holler, J., Bernier, Q., Roberts, J. T., & Robinson, S. A. (2020). Transformational adaptation in least developed countries: Does expanded stakeholder participation make a difference? *Sustainability*, *12*(4), 1657.

Horstmann, B. (2011). Operationalizing the Adaptation Fund: Challenges in allocating funds to the vulnerable. *Climate Policy*, *11*(4), 1086–96.

Huq, S. (2015). Loans or grants for climate finance? *Climate Home News*, 19 October. www.climatechangenews.com/2015/10/19/loans-or-grants-for-climate-finance/.

Huq, S., & Reid, H. (2009). Mainstreaming adaptation in development. *IDS Bulletin*, *35*, 15–21.

IDA (2022). *How are IDA resources allocated?* International Development Association. https://ida.worldbank.org/en/financing/resource-management.

Indian Ministry of Finance (2015). *Climate finance, analysis of a recent OECD report: Some credible facts needed*. Department of Economic Affairs, Ministry of Finance, Government of India. http://pibphoto.nic.in/docu ments/rlink/2015/nov/p2015112901.pdf.

IPCC (1990). *First assessment report climate change: Synthesis*. Intergovernmental Panel on Climate Change. www.ipcc.ch/report/ar1/syr/.

IPCC (1995). *Second assessment report climate change 1995: Synthesis report*. Intergovernmental Panel on Climate Change. www.ipcc.ch/report/ar2/syr/.

IPCC (2001). *Third assessment report climate change 2001: Synthesis report*. Intergovernmental Panel on Climate Change. www.ipcc.ch/report/ar3/syr/.

IPCC (2007). *Fourth assessment report climate change 2007: Synthesis report*. Intergovernmental Panel on Climate Change. www.ipcc.ch/report/ar4/syr/.

IPCC (2012). *Special report on managing the risks of extreme events and disasters to advance climate change adaptation*. Intergovernmental Panel on Climate Change. https://www.ipcc.ch/site/assets/uploads/2018/03/SREX_Full_Report-1.pdf.

IPCC (2014). *Climate change 2014: Impacts, adaptation, and vulnerability*. Intergovernmental Panel on Climate Change. www.ipcc.ch/report/ar5/wg2/.

IPCC (2022). *Climate change 2022: Impacts, adaptation, and vulnerability*. Intergovernmental Panel on Climate Change. www.ipcc.ch/report/sixth-assessment-report-working-group-ii/.

Ishtiaque, A., Estoque, R. C., Eakin, H., Parajuli, J., & Rabby, Y. W. (2022). IPCC's current conceptualization of 'vulnerability' needs more clarification for climate change vulnerability assessments. *Journal of Environmental Management*, *303*, 114246.

Islam, M. M. (2022). Distributive justice in global climate finance: Recipients' climate vulnerability and the allocation of climate funds. *Global Environmental Change, 73*, 102475.

Jacquet, P., & Naudet, J.-D. (2006). Les fondements de l'aide. In Cohen, D., Guillaumont Jeanneney, S., & Jacquet, P. (Eds.). *La France et l'aide publique au développement*. La Documentation française, pp. 47–96.

Jubilee Debt Campaign (2021). *Lower income countries spend five times more on debt payments than dealing with climate change*. https://jubileedebt.org.uk/wp-content/uploads/2021/10/Lower-income-countries-spending-on-adaptation_10.21.pdf.

Junghans, L., & Harmeling, S. (2012). *Different tales from different countries: A first assessment of the OECD 'Adaptation Marker'*. Germanwatch. https://germanwatch.org/en/5375.

Kanbur, R. (2005). Reforming the formula: A modest proposal for introducing development outcomes in IDA allocation procedures. *Revue d'économie du développement, 13*(2–3), 79–108.

Kates, R. W. (2000). Cautionary tales: Adaptation and the global poor. *Climatic Change, 45*, 5–17.

Kelly, P. M., & Adger, W. N. (2000). Theory and practice in assessing vulnerability to climate change and facilitating adaptation. *Climatic Change, 47*(4), 325–52.

Keohane, R. O., & Victor, D. G. (2011). The regime complex for climate change. *Perspectives on Politics, 9*(1), 7–23.

Khan, M. (2014). *Toward a binding climate change adaptation regime: A proposed framework*. Routledge.

Khan, M. (2015). Polluter-pays-principle: The cardinal instrument for addressing climate change. *Laws, 4*(3), 638–53.

Khan, M., & Roberts, J. T. (2013). Adaptation and international climate policy. *Wiley Interdisciplinary Reviews: Climate Change, 4*(3), 171–89.

Khan, M., Robinson, S. A., Weikmans, R., Ciplet, D., & Roberts, J. T. (2020). Twenty-five years of adaptation finance through a climate justice lens. *Climatic Change, 161*(2), 251–69.

Khor, M. (2008). *Developing countries ask for new UNFCCC financial architecture*. Third World Network. www.twn.my/title2/finance/twninfofinance20080601.htm.

Klein, R. J. T. (2009). Identifying countries that are particularly vulnerable to the adverse effects of climate change: An academic or political challenge. *Carbon & Climate Law Review, 3*(3), 284–91.

Klein, R. J. T. (2010). Mainstreaming climate adaptation into development: A policy dilemma. In Ansohn, A., & Pleskovic, B. (Eds.). *Climate governance and development*. World Bank, pp.35–52.

Klein, R. J. T., & Möhner, A. (2011). The political dimension of vulnerability: Implications for the Green Climate Fund. *IDS Bulletin, 42*(3), 15–22.

Klöck, C., Castro, P., Weiler, F., & Blaxekjær, L. Ø. (Eds.). (2021). *Coalitions in the climate change negotiations*. Routledge.

Lahsen, M., & Ribot, J. (2021). Politics of attributing extreme events and disasters to climate change. *Wiley Interdisciplinary Reviews: Climate Change, 13*(1), e750.

Larsen, G., Smith, C., Krishnan, N., Weischer, L., Bartosch, S., & Fekete, H. (2018). *Toward Paris alignment: How the multilateral development banks can better support the Paris Agreement*. World Resources Institute. https://files.wri.org/d8/s3fs-public/toward-paris-alignment_1.pdf

Ledant, J.-P. (2016). Faut-il ajouter une aide climatique ou mieux intégrer les préoccupations climatiques dans l'aide au développement? *Vertigo*. https://doi.org/10.4000/vertigo.17823.

Leiter, T., Olhoff, A., Al Azar, R. et al. (2019). *Adaptation metrics: Current landscape and evolving practices*. Global Center on Adaptation. https://gca.org/reports/adaptation-metrics-current-landscape-and-evolving-practices/.

Lesnikowski, A., Ford, J., Biesbroek, R. et al. (2017). What does the Paris Agreement mean for adaptation? *Climate Policy, 17*(7), 825–31.

Liao, C., Jeffs, N., & Wallace, J. (2022). *What is loss and damage?* Chatham House. www.chathamhouse.org/2022/08/what-loss-and-damage.

LMDCs, & African Group (2021). *Conference room paper: Group of like minded developing countries and the African group of negotiators*. https://unfccc.int/sites/default/files/resource/3_11_21_%20Joint_CPR_New%20Goal.pdf.

Lundsgaarde, E., Adams, K., Dupuy, K. et al. (2021). *The politics of climate finance coordination*. Stockholm Environment Institute. https://cdn.sei.org/wp-content/uploads/2021/10/211015a-burton-shawoo-climate-finance-pb-2109f-final.pdf.

Luxemburg (2020). *Fourth Biennial Report of Luxembourg*. www4.unfccc.int/sites/SubmissionsStaging/NationalReports/Documents/845269310_Luxembourg-BR4-2-BR4_LUX_Final_201123.pdf.

Lynas, M. (2015). The Maldives cannot represent climate leadership with an autocrat at the helm. *The Guardian*, 3 June. www.theguardian.com/environment/2015/jun/03/the-maldives-cannot-represent-climate-leadership-with-an-autocrat-at-the-helm.

Magnan, A. K., & Chalastani, V. I. (2019). *Towards a global adaptation progress tracker: First thoughts*. IDDRI Sustainable Development & International Relations. https://bit.ly/2lMCdrU.

Magnan, A. K., & Ribera, T. (2016). Global adaptation after Paris. *Science, 352*(6291), 1280–2.

Magnan, A. K., Schipper, E. L. F., Burkett, M. et al. (2016). Addressing the risk of maladaptation to climate change. *Wiley Interdisciplinary Reviews: Climate Change, 7*(5), 646–65.

Martinez-Alier, J. (2003). *The environmentalism of the poor: A study of ecological conflicts and valuation*. Edward Elgar.

McGinn, A., & Isenhour, C. (2021). Negotiating the future of the Adaptation Fund: On the politics of defining and defending justice in the post-Paris Agreement period. *Climate Policy, 21*(3), 383–95.

McGray, H., Hammill, A., Bradley, R., Schipper, L., & Parry, J. E. (2007). *Weathering the storm: Options for framing adaptation and development*. World Resources Institute.

MDB Joint Report (2021). *2020 joint report on multilateral development banks' climate finance*. www.ebrd.com/cs/Satellite?c=Content&cid=139529936 6792&d=&pagename=EBRD%2FContent%2FDownloadDocument.

Michaelowa, K., Michaelowa, A., Reinsberg, B., & Shishlov, I. (2020). Do multilateral development bank trust funds allocate climate finance efficiently? *Sustainability, 12*(14), 5529.

Monheim, K. (2014). *How effective negotiation management promotes multilateral cooperation: The power of process in climate, trade, and biosafety negotiations*. Routledge.

Muccione, V., Allen, S. K., Huggel, C., & Birkmann, J. (2017). Differentiating regions for adaptation financing: The role of global vulnerability and risk distributions. *Wiley Interdisciplinary Reviews: Climate Change, 8*(2), e447.

Müller, B. (2011). Time to roll up the sleeves: Even higher! Longer-term climate finance after Cancun. *Environmental Liability, 1*, 3–7.

Müller, B. (2015). *The Paris predictability problem: What to do about climate finance for the 2020 climate agreement?* Oxford Climate Policy. https://oxfordclimatepolicy.org/sites/default/files/The_Paris_Predictability_Problem_published.pdf.

Müller, B., Sharma, A., Gomez-Echeverri, L., Rook, D. P., & Chandani, A. (2010). *The reformed financial mechanism of the UNFCCC, Part II: The question of oversight*. Oxford Institute for Energy Studies. https://oxford climatepolicy.org/sites/default/files/EV52_0_0.pdf.

Müller B., & Winkler, H. (2008). *One step forward, two steps back? The governance of the World Bank Climate Investment Funds*. Oxford Institute for Energy Studies. https://a9w7k6q9.stackpathcdn.com/wpcms/wp-content/uploads/2011/01/Feb-2008-GovernanceoftheWorldBankClimateInvestmentFunds-Benito MüllerandHaraldWinkler.pdf

Naudet, J.-D. (2000). L'aide extérieure est-elle un instrument de justice? Une analyse des évolutions des fondements éthiques de l'aide au développement. *L'Économie Politique*, (7), 71–85.

Naudet, J.-D. (2006). Les OMD et l'aide de cinquième génération: analyse de l'évolution des fondements éthiques de l'aide au développement. *Afrique contemporaine*, 2, 141–74.

Naudet, J.-D., Severino, J.-M., & Charnoz, O. (2007). Aide internationale: vers une justice sociale globale? *Esprit*, 5, 101–11.

NDC Partnership (2022). *Climate finance explorer.* https://ndcpartnership.org/climate-finance-explorer.

O'Brien, K., Eriksen, S., Nygaard, L. P., & Schjolden, A. N. E. (2007). Why different interpretations of vulnerability matter in climate change discourses. *Climate Policy*, 7(1), 73–88.

OECD (2019). *Aligning development co-operation and climate action: The only way forward.* Organisation for Economic Co-operation and Development. https://doi.org/10.1787/5099ad91-en.

OECD (2021a). *Climate finance provided and mobilised by developed countries: Aggregate trends updated with 2019 data.* Organisation for Economic Cooperation and Development. https://doi.org/10.1787/03590fb7-en.

OECD (2021b). *Integrating environmental and climate action into development co-operation.* Organisation for Economic Cooperation and Development. https://doi.org/10.1787/285905b2-en.

OECD (2022). *Climate finance provided and mobilised by developed countries in 2016–2020: Insights from disaggregated analysis.* Organisation for Economic Cooperation and Development. https://doi.org/10.1787/286dae5d-en.

OECD & UNDP (2019). *Making development co-operation more effective: 2019 progress report.* Organisation for Economic Cooperation and Development and United Nations Development Programme. https://doi.org/10.1787/26f2638f-en.

OECD DAC (2006). *Declaration on integrating climate change adaptation into development co-operation.* Development Assistance Committee of the Organisation for Economic Cooperation and Development. www.oecd.org/dac/environment-development/44229637.pdf.

OECD DAC (2021a). *OECD DAC declaration on a new approach to align development co-operation with the goals of the Paris Agreement on climate change.* Development Assistance Committee of the Organisation for Economic Cooperation and Development. www.oecd.org/dac/development-assistance-committee/dac-declaration-climate-change-cop26.pdf.

OECD DAC (2021b). *What is ODA?* Development Assistance Committee of the Organisation for Economic Cooperation and Development. www.oecd

.org/dac/financing-sustainable-development/development-finance-standards/ What-is-ODA.pdf.

Opeskin, B. (1996). The moral foundations of foreign aid. *World Development*, *24*, 21–44.

Orlove, B. (2022). The concept of adaptation. *Annual Review of Environment and Resources*, *47*(1), 535–581.

Oxfam (2007). *Adapting to climate change: What is needed in poor countries and who should pay?* https://oxfamilibrary.openrepository.com/bitstream/ handle/10546/114075/bp104-adapting-to-climate-change-290507-en.pdf? sequence=1.

Oxfam (2012). *The climate 'fiscal cliff': An evaluation of fast start finance and lessons for the future.* https://oxfamilibrary.openrepository.com/bitstream/ handle/10546/253332/ib-climate-fiscal-cliff-media-briefing-251112-en.pdf? sequence=1.

Oxfam (2020). *Climate finance shadow report 2020.* https://oxfamilibrary.open repository.com/bitstream/handle/10546/621066/bp-climate-finance-shadow-report-2020-201020-en.pdf.

Palutikof, J., Parry, M., Smith, M. S. et al. (2013). The past, present and future of adaptation: Setting the context and naming the challenges. In Palutikof, J., Boulter, S. L., Ash, A. J. et al. (Eds.). *Climate adaptation futures*. John Wiley, pp. 3–29.

Parry, M., Arnell, N., Berry, P. et al. (2009). *A review of the UNFCCC and other recent estimates*. Grantham Institute for Climate Change and International Institute for Environment and Development. https://pubs.iied.org/sites/ default/files/pdfs/migrate/11501IIED.pdf.

Pauw, W. P. (2017). Mobilising private adaptation finance: Developed country perspectives. *International Environmental Agreements: Politics, Law and Economics*, *17*(1), 55–71.

Pauw, P., Grünng, C., & Menzel, C. (2020). *Number of beneficiaries as an indicator for adaptation: Do the numbers add up?* 2nd ed. GCF Monitor, FS-UNEP Centre for Climate & Sustainable Energy Finance. www.fs-unep-centre.org/wp-content/uploads/2020/04/GCFMonitor-edition2-final.pdf.

Pauw, P., Mbeva, K., & Van Asselt, H. (2019). Subtle differentiation of countries' responsibilities under the Paris Agreement. *Palgrave Communications*, *5*(1), 1–7.

Pauw, P., Moslener, U., Zamarioli, L. et al. (2022). Post-2025 climate finance target: How much more and how much better? *Climate Policy*, *22*(9–10), 1241–1251. https://doi.org/10.1080/14693062.2022.2114985.

Persson, A., & Remling, E. (2014). Equity and efficiency in adaptation finance: Initial experiences of the Adaptation Fund. *Climate Policy*, *14*, 488–506.

Pickering, J., & Barry, C. (2012). On the concept of climate debt: Its moral and political value. *Critical Review of International Social and Political Philosophy, 15*(5), 667–85.

Pickering, J., Betzold, C., & Skovgaard, J. (2017). Managing fragmentation and complexity in the emerging system of international climate finance. *International Environmental Agreements: Politics, Law and Economics, 17*(1), 1–16.

Pickering, J., Skovgaard, J., Kim, S. et al. (2015). Acting on climate finance pledges: Inter-agency dynamics and relationships with aid in contributor states. *World Development, 68,* 149–62.

Project Catalyst (2009). *Adaptation to climate change: Potential costs and choices for a global agreement. Findings of the Adaptation Working Group of Project Catalyst.* Climate Works Foundation.

Raman, M. (2021). *COP 25 ends amidst major north-south differences.* Briefing Paper. Third World Network. www.twn.my/title2/climate/doc/Briefing%20paper%20COP25.pdf.

Remling, E., & Persson, Å. (2015). Who is adaptation for? Vulnerability and adaptation benefits in proposals approved by the UNFCCC Adaptation Fund. *Climate and Development, 7*(1), 16–34.

Ribot, J. (2010). Vulnerability does not fall from the sky: Toward multiscale, pro-poor climate policy. In Mearns, R., & Norton, A. (Eds.). *Social dimensions of climate change: Equity and vulnerability in a warming world.* World Bank, 47–74.

Roberts, J. T., & Parks, B. (2006). *A climate of injustice: Global inequality, north-south politics, and climate policy.* MIT Press.

Roberts, J. T., & Parks, B. (2016). *A climate of injustice: Global inequality, north-south politics, and climate policy.* MIT Press

Roberts, T., & Weikmans, R. (2015). *The unfinished agenda of the Paris climate talks: Finance to the global south.* Brookings Planet Policy. www.brookings.edu/blog/planetpolicy/2015/12/22/the-unfinished-agenda-of-the-paris-climate-talks-finance-to-the-global-south/.

Roberts, J. T., & Weikmans, R. (2017). Postface: Fragmentation, failing trust and enduring tensions over what counts as climate finance. *International Environmental Agreements: Politics, Law and Economics, 17*(1), 129–37.

Roberts, J. T., Hite, A. B., & Chorev, N. (Eds.). (2014). *The globalization and development reader: Perspectives on development and global change.* John Wiley.

Roberts, J. T., Weikmans, R., & Jones, C. (2017). Allocating climate adaptation finance: Shifting positions in the scholarly and policy realms. *Conference: The emerging complexity of climate adaptation governance in a globalising.* Stockholm Environment Institute and Stockholm University, 23–24 May.

https://dipot.ulb.ac.be/dspace/bitstream/2013/262635/3/RobertsWeikmans andJones2017.pdf.

Roberts, J. T., Weikmans, R., Robinson, S. A. et al. (2021). Rebooting a failed promise of climate finance. *Nature Climate Change, 11*(3), 180–2.

Robertsen, J., Francken, N., & Molenaers, N. (2015). *Determinants of the flow of bilateral adaptation-related climate change financing to Sub-Saharan African countries.* LICOS Discussion Paper 373. Catholic University Leuven.

Robinson, S. A., & Dornan, M. (2017). International financing for climate change adaptation in small island developing states. *Regional Environmental Change, 17*(4), 1103–15.

Rothstein, R. L. (2015). *Global bargaining: UNCTAD and the quest for a new international economic order.* Princeton University Press.

Saunders, N. (2019). *Climate change adaptation finance: Are the most vulnerable nations prioritised?* Stockholm Environment Institute. www.sei.org/wp-content/uploads/2019/04/climate-change-adaptation-finance-are-the-most-vulnerable-nations-prioritised.pdf.

Schalatek, L., Nakhooda, S., & Barnard, S. (2012). *Climate finance thematic briefing: Adaptation finance.* Overseas Development Institute and Heinrich Böll Stiftung North America.

Schipper, E. L. F. (2006). Conceptual history of adaptation in the UNFCCC process. *Review of European Community & International Environmental Law, 15*, 82–92.

Schipper, L., & Pelling, M. (2006). Disaster risk, climate change and international development: Scope for, and challenges to, integration. *Disasters, 30*(1), 19–38.

Schipper, L., Tanner, T., Dube, O. P., Adams, K. M., & Huq, S. (2020). The debate: Is global development adapting to climate change? *World Development Perspectives, 18*, 100205.

Seballos, F., & Kreft, S. (2011). Towards an understanding of the political economy of the PPCR. *IDS Bulletin, 42*(3), 33–41.

Shalal, A. (2021). IMF eyes new trust to provide aid to broader group of countries-Georgieva. *Reuters*, 13 June. www.reuters.com/business/exclusive-imf-exploring-creation-new-trust-provide-sdrs-broader-group-countries-2021-06-13/.

Shankland, A., & Chambote, R. (2011). Prioritising PPCR investments in Mozambique: The politics of 'country ownership' and 'stakeholder participation'. *IDS Bulletin, 42*(3), 62–9.

Sharma, J., & Ravindranath, N. H. (2019). Applying IPCC 2014 framework for hazard-specific vulnerability assessment under climate change. *Environmental Research Communications, 1*(5), 051004.

Sharma-Khushal, S., Schalatek, L., Singh, H., & White, H. (2022). *The loss and damage finance facility: Why and how*. Christian Aid. www.christianaid.org .uk/sites/default/files/2022-05/The-Loss-and-Damage-Finance-Facility.pdf.

Singh, H., & Bose, I. (2021). *Artificial distinction between climate change adaptation and development restricts access to climate finance for developing countries*. Henrich Böll Stiftung. https://us.boell.org/en/2021/06/30/artificial-distinction-between-climate-change-adaptation-and-development-restricts.

Sperling, F. (2003). *Poverty and climate change: Reducing the vulnerability of the poor through adaptation*. AfDB, ADB, DFID, BMZ, DGIS, OECD, UNDP, UNEP, and World Bank. www.oecd.org/env/cc/2502872.pdf.

Stadelmann, M., Roberts, J. T., & Michaelowa, A. (2011). New and additional to what? Assessing options for baselines to assess climate finance pledges. *Climate and Development, 3*, 175–92.

Stadelmann, M., Persson, Å., Ratajczak-Juszko, I., & Michaelowa, A. (2014). Equity and cost-effectiveness of multilateral adaptation finance: Are they friends or foes? *International Environmental Agreements: Politics, Law and Economics, 14*(2), 101–20.

Stern, N. (2007). *The economics of climate change: The Stern review*. Cambridge University Press.

Swaziland (2013). *Submission by Swaziland on behalf of the African Group on adaptation in the 2015 Agreement*. https://unfccc.int/files/documentation/ submissions_from_parties/adp/application/pdf/adp_african_group_work stream_1_adaptation_20131008.pdf.

Sweden (2019). *Sweden's fourth Biennial Report*. https://unfccc.int/sites/ default/files/resource/Fourth%20Biennial%20report_%20Sweden.pdf.

Tandon, A. (2021). Climate change not the main driver of Madagascar food crisis, scientists find. *Carbon Brief*, 1 December. www.carbonbrief.org/ climate-change-not-the-main-driver-of-madagascar-food-crisis-scientists-find.

Tanner, T., & Allouche, J. (2011). Towards a new political economy of climate change and development. *IDS Bulletin, 42*(3), 1–14.

Task Force on Climate, Development and the IMF (2021). *Re-channeling special drawing rights for a climate resilient and just transition*. www.bu .edu/gdp/files/2021/10/TF_Policy-Brief_FIN.pdf.

Tellam, I., Ali, S., Ahmed, A. et al. (2018). *Climate adaptation finance govern- ance standards*. Transparency International. https://images.transparencycdn .org/images/2018_Report_AdaptionGovernanceStandards_English.pdf.

Thomas, A., & Theokritoff, E. (2021). Debt-for-climate swaps for small islands. *Nature Climate Change, 11*(11), 889–91.

Tubiana, L., Magnan, A., & Gemenne, F. (2010). *Anticiper pour s'adapter: le nouvel enjeu du changement climatique*. Pearson Education France.

UK Independent Commission for Aid Impact (2021). *UK aid's alignment with the Paris Agreement: A rapid review.* https://icai.independent.gov.uk/wp-content/uploads/UK-aids-alignment-with-the-Paris-agreement_ICAI-review.pdf.

UNDP (2007). *Human development report 2007/2008.* United Nations Development Programme.http://hdr.undp.org/sites/default/files/reports/268/hdr_20072008_en_complete.pdf.

UNEP (2014). *The adaptation gap report 2014.* United Nations Environment Programme. https://wedocs.unep.org/bitstream/handle/20.500.11822/9331/-Adaptation_gap_report_a_prel.pdf?sequence=2&isAllowed=y

UNEP (2016). *The adaptation finance gap report.* United Nations Environment Programme. https://wedocs.unep.org/bitstream/handle/20.500.11822/32865/agr2016.pdf?sequence=1&isAllowed=y

UNEP (2017). *The adaptation gap report 2017.* United Nations Environment Programme. https://wedocs.unep.org/bitstream/handle/20.500.11822/22172/adaptation_gap_2017.pdf?sequence=1&isAllowed=y.

UNEP (2021). *Adaptation gap report 2021.* United Nations Environment Programme. www.unep.org/resources/adaptation-gap-report-2021.

UNFCCC (1992). *United Nations Framework Convention on Climate Change.* https://unfccc.int/resource/docs/convkp/conveng.pdf.

UNFCCC (2001a). *Decision 10/CP.7: Funding under the Kyoto Protocol.* United Nations Framework Convention on Climate Change. https://unfccc.int/sites/default/files/resource/docs/cop7/13a01.pdf.

UNFCCC (2001b). *Decision 28/CP.7: Guidelines for the preparation of national adaptation programmes of action.* United Nations Framework Convention on Climate Change. https://unfccc.int/resource/ldc/documents/13a04p7.pdf.

UNFCCC (2007). *Decision 1/CMP.3: Adaptation Fund.* United Nations Framework Convention on Climate Change. https://unfccc.int/sites/default/files/resource/docs/2007/cmp3/eng/09a01.pdf.

UNFCCC (2008). *Decision 1/CMP.4: Adaptation Fund.* United Nations Framework Convention on Climate Change. https://unfccc.int/resource/docs/2008/cmp4/eng/11a02.pdf#page=1.

UNFCCC (2009). *Decision 2/CP.15: Copenhagen Accord.* United Nations Framework Convention on Climate Change. https://unfccc.int/resource/docs/2009/cop15/eng/11a01.pdf.

UNFCCC (2010). *Decision 1/CP.16: The Cancun Agreements.* United Nations Framework Convention on Climate Change. https://unfccc.int/resource/docs/2010/cop16/eng/07a01.pdf.

UNFCCC (2011). *Decision 5/CP.17: National adaptation plans.* United Nations Framework Convention on Climate Change. https://unfccc.int/files/

adaptation/cancun_adaptation_framework/national_adaptation_plans/application/pdf/decision_5_cp_17.pdf.

UNFCCC (2015). *Decision 1/CP.21: Adoption of the Paris Agreement*. United Nations Framework Convention on Climate Change. https://unfccc.int/resource/docs/2015/cop21/eng/10a01.pdf.

UNFCCC (2018a). *Decision 4/CP.24: Report of the Standing Committee on Finance*. United Nations Framework Convention on Climate Change. https://unfccc.int/sites/default/files/resource/10a1.pdf.

UNFCCC (2018b). *Decision 13/CMA.1: Matters relating to the Adaptation Fund*. United Nations Framework Convention on Climate Change. https://unfccc.int/sites/default/files/resource/cma2018_3_add2_new_advance.pdf.

UNFCCC (2018c). *Decision 18/CMA.1: Modalities, procedures and guidelines for the transparency framework for action and support referred to in Article 13 of the Paris Agreement*. United Nations Framework Convention on Climate Change. https://unfccc.int/sites/default/files/resource/CMA2018_03a02E.pdf.

UNFCCC (2021). *Decision -/CP.26: Glasgow Climate Pact*. United Nations Framework Convention on Climate Change. https://unfccc.int/sites/default/files/resource/cop26_auv_2f_cover_decision.pdf.

UNFCCC SCF (2018). *2018 biennial assessment and overview of climate finance flows*. UNFCCC Standing Committee on Finance. https://unfccc.int/sites/default/files/resource/2018%20BA%20Technical%20Report%20Final%20Feb%202019.pdf.

UNFCCC SCF (2021a). *2020 biennial assessment and overview of climate finance flows*. UNFCCC Standing Committee on Finance. https://unfccc.int/sites/default/files/resource/54307_1%20-%20UNFCCC%20BA%202020%20-%20Report%20-%20V4.pdf.

UNFCCC SCF (2021b). *First report on the determination of the needs of developing country parties related to implementing the Convention and the Paris Agreement*. UNFCCC Standing Committee on Finance. https://unfccc.int/sites/default/files/resource/54307_2%20-%20UNFCCC%20First%20NDR%20technical%20report%20-%20web%20%28004%29.pdf.

UNFCCC Secretariat (2007). *Investment and financial flows to address climate change*. https://unfccc.int/resource/docs/publications/financial_flows.pdf.

UNFCCC Secretariat (2020). *Compilation and synthesis of fourth biennial reports of parties included in Annex I to the Convention*. https://unfccc.int/sites/default/files/resource/sbi2020_inf10_rev01.pdf.

van Gameren, V., Weikmans, R., & Zaccai, E. (2014). *L'adaptation au changement climatique*. Éditions La Découverte.

Vanhala, L., & Hestbaek, C. (2016). Framing climate change loss and damage in UNFCCC negotiations. *Global Environmental Politics*, *16*(4), 111–29.

Vidal, J. (2009). Copenhagen: Head of African bloc calls on poorer nations to compromise over climate funding. *The Guardian*, 16 December. www .theguardian.com/environment/2009/dec/16/meles-zenawi-copenhagen-climate-funding.

Vihma, A., Mulugetta, Y., & Karlsson-Vinkhuyzen, S. (2011). Negotiating solidarity? The G77 through the prism of climate change negotiations. *Global Change, Peace & Security*, *23*(3), 315–34.

Weikmans, R. (2012). Le coût de l'adaptation aux changements climatiques dans les pays en développement. *Vertigo*, *12*(1). https://doi.org/10.4000/ vertigo.11931.

Weikmans, R. (2013). Du changement incrémental au changement transformationnel: actions de l'aide internationale à l'adaptation. *Actes du 1er Congrès interdisciplinaire du Développement Durable: quelle transition pour nos sociétés?* thème 5, pp. 105–24.

Weikmans, R. (2015). *Le financement international de l'adaptation au changement climatique: quelle vision de l'aide au développement?* Thèse de doctorat. Université Libre de Bruxelles.

Weikmans, R. (2016a). Dimensions éthiques de l'allocation du financement international de l'adaptation au changement climatique. *Vertigo*, *16*(2). https://doi.org/10.4000/vertigo.17677

Weikmans, R. (2016b). Le rôle de la coopération au développement dans le financement international de l'adaptation. In Zacharie, A. (Ed.). *La nouvelle géographie du développement, Coopérer dans un monde en mutation*. La Muette, pp. 175–85.

Weikmans, R. (2017). Comprendre la mobilisation financière autour de l'aide à l'adaptation au changement climatique. *Critique internationale*, *4*(77), 121–39.

Weikmans, R. (2018). Évaluation de l'aide et mobilisation financière internationale autour de l'adaptation au changement climatique. *Revue internationale des études du développement*, *2*(234), 151–75.

Weikmans, R., & Gupta, A. (2021). Assessing state compliance with multilateral climate transparency requirements. *Climate Policy*, *21*(5), 635–51.

Weikmans, R., & Roberts, J. T. (2016). *Fit for purpose: Negotiating the new climate finance accounting systems*. Policy Brief 3. Climate Strategies. https://climatestrategies.org/wp-content/uploads/2016/05/CS-Fit-for-Purpose-Climate-Finance-Accounting-formatted-09.05.2016.pdf.

Weikmans, R., & Roberts, J. T. (2018). *It's déjà vu all over again: Climate finance at COP24*. Brookings Planet Policy. www.brookings.edu/blog/ planetpolicy/2018/12/06/its-deja-vu-all-over-again-climate-finance-at-cop24/.

Weikmans, R., & Roberts, J. T. (2019). The international climate finance accounting muddle: Is there hope on the horizon? *Climate and Development, 11*(2), 97–111.

Weikmans, R., & Zaccai, E. (2017). Pourquoi aider les pays en développement? Conceptions de la justice dans l'aide à l'adaptation au changement climatique. *Développement durable et territoires, 8*(1). https://doi.org/10.4000/developpementdurable.11668

Weikmans, R., Asselt, H. V., & Roberts, J. T. (2020a). Transparency requirements under the Paris Agreement and their (un) likely impact on strengthening the ambition of nationally determined contributions (NDCs). *Climate Policy, 20*(4), 511–26.

Weikmans, R., Roberts, J. T., & Robinson, S. A. (2020b). What counts as climate finance? Define urgently. *Nature, 588*(7837), 220.

Weikmans, R., Roberts, J. T., Baum, J., Bustos, M. C., & Durand, A. (2017). Assessing the credibility of how climate adaptation aid projects are categorised. *Development in Practice, 27*(4), 458–71.

Weiler, F., Klöck, C., & Dornan, M. (2018). Vulnerability, good governance, or donor interests? The allocation of aid for climate change adaptation. *World Development, 104*, 65–77.

World Bank (2006). *Investment framework for clean energy and development.* http://web.worldbank.org/archive/website01021/WEB/IMAGES/DC2006-2.PDF.

World Bank (2009). *The costs to developing countries of adapting to climate change.* https://reliefweb.int/sites/reliefweb.int/files/resources/14D99A1A0 3815EC4492576470019CCED-WB_sep2009.pdf.

World Bank (2022). *Adaptation Fund Trust Fund: Financial report prepared by the trustee.* https://fiftrustee.worldbank.org/content/dam/fif/funds/adapt/TrusteeReports/AF%20Trustee%20Report%20at%20June%2030%202022.pdf.

World Bank Open Data (2022). *GDP per capita.* https://data.worldbank.org/indicator/NY.GDP.PCAP.CD.

Zacharie, A. (2013). *Mondialisation: qui gagne et qui perd – Essai sur l'économie politique du développement.* Éditions Le Bord de l'Eau.

Zamarioli, L. H., Pauw, P., König, M., & Chenet, H. (2021). The climate consistency goal and the transformation of global finance. *Nature Climate Change, 11*(7), 578–83.

Acknowledgements

I acknowledge the publications where earlier versions of this Element's Sections appeared. Parts of Section 2 were published in Weikmans (*Critique internationale*, 2017). A portion of Section 3 was published in Weikmans and Zaccai (*Développement durable et territoires*, 2017). Section 4 partially draws on Weikmans (*Vertigo*, 2016a). Parts of Section 5 are based on Weikmans (*Revue internationale des études du développement*, 2018). This work was supported by the Academy of Finland under grant number 333127.

About the Author

Romain Weikmans is Senior Research Fellow at the Finnish Institute of International Affairs and Adjunct Professor at the Université Libre de Bruxelles/ Free University of Brussels. His main research interests centre on international climate finance, climate transparency, and climate adaptation.

Cambridge Elements ☰

Earth System Governance

Frank Biermann
Utrecht University

Frank Biermann is Research Professor of Global Sustainability Governance with the Copernicus Institute of Sustainable Development, Utrecht University, the Netherlands. He is the founding Chair of the Earth System Governance Project, a global transdisciplinary research network launched in 2009; and Editor-in-Chief of the new peer-reviewed journal *Earth System Governance* (Elsevier). In April 2018, he won a European Research Council Advanced Grant for a research program on the steering effects of the Sustainable Development Goals.

Aarti Gupta
Wageningen University

Aarti Gupta is Professor of Global Environmental Governance at Wageningen University, The Netherlands. She is Lead Faculty and a member of the Scientific Steering Committee of the Earth System Governance (ESG) Project and a Coordinating Lead Author of its 2018 Science and Implementation Plan. She is also principal investigator of the Dutch Research Council-funded TRANSGOV project on the Transformative Potential of Transparency in Climate Governance. She holds a PhD from Yale University in environmental studies.

Michael Mason
London School of Economics and Political Science (LSE)

Michael Mason is Associate Professor in the Department of Geography and Environment at the London School of Economics and Political Science (LSE). At LSE he also Director of the Middle East Centre and an Associate of the Grantham Institute on Climate Change and the Environment. Alongside his academic research on environmental politics and governance, he has advised various governments and international organisations on environmental policy issues, including the European Commission, ICRC, NATO, the UK Government (FCDO) and UNDP.

About the Series

Linked with the Earth System Governance Project, this exciting new series will provide concise but authoritative studies of the governance of complex socio-ecological systems, written by world-leading scholars. Highly interdisciplinary in scope, the series will address governance processes and institutions at all levels of decision-making, from local to global, within a planetary perspective that seeks to align current institutions and governance systems with the fundamental 21st Century challenges of global environmental change and earth system transformations.

Elements in this series will present cutting edge scientific research, while also seeking to contribute innovative transformative ideas towards better governance. A key aim of the series is to present policy-relevant research that is of interest to both academics and policy-makers working on earth system governance.

More information about the Earth System Governance project can be found at:
www.earthsystemgovernance.org

Cambridge Elements $\equiv$

Earth System Governance

Elements in the Series

Printed in the United States
by Baker & Taylor Publisher Services